The Satiric
JOHN TRL

THE PROGRESS OF DULNESS
and M'FINGAL

With Illustrations from Engravings by E. TISDALE
Edited with a Preface and Notes by
EDWIN T. BOWDEN

UNIVERSITY OF TEXAS PRESS
AUSTIN

LIBRARY OF CONGRESS CATALOG CARD NUMBER 61–15829

.

PRINTED & BOUND IN THE UNITED STATES OF AMERICA

TABLE

OF

CONTENTS

EDITOR'S PREFACE

&

A NOTE ON THE TEXT

THERE ARE MANY REASONS FOR MAKING THE SATIRIC POEMS of John Trumbull again available to the reading public, but one of the greatest is their continued ability to amuse. The poems are as entertaining as any that American literature has produced. Of course they are of interest too as America's first good poetic satires, or as representative examples of the best of America's new national literature of the eighteenth century, or as historical documents illustrating the thoughts and emotions and problems of the time. But for the most part they are just amusing to read, now as in the time when they were still new and fresh and immediate and perhaps a little shocking. If they are no longer new and shocking, they are still surprisingly fresh, for our taste in wit has not changed that much and Trumbull's has a quality that speaks to any period. And more often than we have any right to ask, they are still immediate, sometimes admittedly through an act of the reader's imagination, but often enough because they talk of the same human problems that plague us today.

Looking back at John Trumbull the man, there is little reason to suspect this lasting quality of his mind; certainly it does not appear particularly in his public life. He was born in 1750 in one of those Connecticut families that deservedly was thought to represent solidity and achievement, public service and private ability. He seems to have been a rather delicate boy whose mind made up for whatever his body may have lacked. He even performed the astonishing feat of passing the Yale College examination for admission at the age of seven, although he wisely waited six more years before entering the college. Once he did enter, he remained for nine apparently contented years as student, as bachelor, and then as tutor, in all three positions coming to know perhaps too well the curriculum and the attitudes that he was to attack in *The Progress of Dulness* written during his last years in the college. Just after concluding the final section of that poem in 1773 he moved to Boston as a student of the law, the profession he was to pursue for the rest of his life. There he studied in the office of John Adams and came to know other revolutionary leaders during the period of the Boston Tea Party and the Boston Port Bill. He was already gathering information and thoughts for the *M'Fingal* that was to follow, even though he did not know it then. At best he seems to have been a temperate patriot in a time of patriotic intemperance. (It is no wonder that Kenneth Roberts chooses to mention him on the first page of *Oliver Wiswell*, a novel of the Revolution told from the Tory point of view.) By 1774 affairs in Boston were becoming too tempestuous, and he returned to New Haven to practice law, remaining in Connecticut, as it turned out, until his seventy-fifth year. *M'Fingal* was his anonymous contribution to the war, for he did not serve in the army and in 1777 even timorously left New Haven when it seemed in danger of invasion, moving first to Westbury and then to Hartford. In these years he held a number of distinguished offices: attorney for the county of Hartford, member of the state legislature, judge of the state superior court, judge of the supreme court of errors in Connecticut. A good, conservative Federalist, he served in his offices with the decency expected of a

Trumbull. Late in his life he retired from public office and in 1825 went to Detroit to live with his daughter, the wife of the governor of Michigan, for his last six years.

It is unfair, however, to look only at his public life, for the world today is interested not in John Trumbull the solid citizen of Connecticut but in John Trumbull the poet. As a satirist of his times, however, and a poet of the American revolution, it is difficult to make the distinction between poet and man of public life that the next age was to believe in. It is particularly difficult with Trumbull, for he not only wrote of public affairs like many others, but he was also numbered among the "Connecticut Wits," an informal association of New England poets that were generally thought—and certainly thought themselves—the first representatives of a new, native American literature. With such a dignified and public literary position to uphold, the "Pleiades of Connecticut" could hardly be allowed to withdraw into any private, poetic retreat. And none seemed to want to, for all combined with their heavy public position as American poets a further public position as men of affairs. The humorless Timothy Dwight, author of *Greenfield Hill* and *The Conquest of Canäan,* was a minister and president of Yale College. Joel Barlow, *The Hasty Pudding, The Columbiad,* was a diplomat. Lemuel Hopkins was a physician; Theodore Dwight, like Trumbull, a lawyer; David Humphreys, a diplomat and breeder of merino sheep. Other and lesser members were similarly good citizens of the community and joined with equal enthusiasm the attempt to create a public poetry—properly conservative in thought and method—that would make America and the new United States an official and recognized site in the community of letters.

It seems fair to say, however, that of the group John Trumbull was the one member with a natural mind for poetry and a genuine feeling for literature as an art. His biographer Alexander Cowie—whose *John Trumbull: Connecticut Wit* (1936) is the finest and most complete single work on Trumbull—records that young John began to compose verses at the age of four (he had already read the entire

Bible), although he waited until he was five before he began
to write them out. By his senior year in college he was turning
out verses with apparent facility, and they clearly marked his
bent: the serious pieces that have survived are generally competent and lifeless; the humorous pieces, lively and promising. At the same time that he began trying his hand at verse
with some degree of success, he began too a series of essays
in the newspapers. "The Meddler" was his first attempt,
published in *The Boston Chronicle* in 1769 and 1770 as a
series of Addisonian essays with something of the satiric wit
that Trumbull was increasingly to develop. These were soon
followed in 1770 and in 1773 by a much more biting series,
"The Correspondent," in *The Connecticut Journal.* Here
Trumbull was more pointed and personal in his satire, particularly aiming his strokes at certain doctrines and divines,
for his interests, as befitted a young scholar at Yale, were still
caught up in large part in divinity.

The exercise of his satiric wit was a good beginning for
Trumbull, even if prose was to prove a false start. Except
for his Master's oration of 1770, *An Essay on the Use and
Advantages of the Fine Arts*—a work properly academic but
containing a protest against the conservative curriculum of
Yale College that he was to make better known in *The Progress of Dulness*—he published no more prose of interest to
the literary historian. In the meantime he continued to write
verse, and a few of the earlier poems are of greater interest
than simply the biographical. "Epithalamium," 1769, published in an expurgated version some thirty-five years later,
is an amusing parody and burlesque in the traditional genre
of the wedding song, written on the occasion of the marriage
of a college tutor. It lost Trumbull the friendship of the tutor
—as his writing was always so apt to do—but it must have
increased his reputation as a wit. "Advice to Ladies of a
Certain Age," 1771, finally published in the collected works
of 1820, is caustic advice, as might be expected, and verges
on the satiric. Perhaps one other published poem should be
mentioned, if only for contrast: "An Elegy on the Times,"
1774. The poem, on the occasion of the Boston Port Bill, is

a forecast of the patriotism of *M'Fingal* to follow, but is so prudently conservative that the historical patriot finds little excitement in it, and so dignified and proper that the admirer of Trumbull's witty satire finds little interest. Like so many comic poets, Trumbull would keep trying to be serious.

Whatever biographical interest these early poems may have, Trumbull's reputation must stand on the two longer works here reprinted. For the earlier poetry is often readable, but probably not enough to keep his name alive. And after the appearance of the complete *M'Fingal* in 1782, Trumbull published almost no poetry except for his collaboration with other Connecticut Wits in *The Anarchiad,* 1786–87, and *The Echo,* 1791–1805, not very exciting newspaper satires on issues of the day. It seems now that he may also have published some "carrier's addresses" in the 1780's, poems designed to be distributed by newspaper carriers on New Year's day. Historically he cannot be called a "two poem man," yet that is the impression he offers the modern reader. It is hardly fair, however, to attack Trumbull for not being a more consistent or a more prolific or a more dedicated poet than he was. Even if his was only a minor talent when compared to that of the great poets of the world, it is an interesting and an entertaining and a competent talent that did offer two fine long satiric poems that can still hold the amused attention of the reader in the second century after their publication. Perhaps by the very definition of the term that is not so minor after all.

The Progress of Dulness, 1773, has from its first publication attracted less attention than *M'Fingal,* although it is in many ways the more readable of the two today. For the period during and after the Revolution it did not have the nationalistic or historical immediacy to hold the same attraction, and the next age to some extent simply accepted the reputation given the poems by the earlier. At first glance too *The Progress of Dulness* seems more dated than *M'Fingal:* the poem of the Revolution is about past events, of course, but events so clearly past that they cause no confusion and offer a certain historical interest. *The Progress of Dulness* is

in many respects about the same problems and the same
crotchets of human nature that exist today, but it uses a
tradition and a vocabulary that belong to the past and presents characters drawn from the literary conventions of the
eighteenth century that may seem quaintly archaic. The
reader today is liable to a certain confusion, a little like that
engendered by eating lunch in an olde tea shoppe beside the
superhighway. But after the first glance, the poem begins to
speak directly to the modern reader as he recognizes in Trumbull's Tom, Dick and Harriet the friends or relatives or class-
mates he knows for himself. Even if we no longer call our
gay young men "fops" or our silly girls "coquettes," we recognize in the eighteenth century types—for all their ruffles and
tuckers—the human being that is still with us. And if the details of our formal education and our college curriculum
have changed since Trumbull's day, we still recognize the
college's reluctance to leave the old and the tried, and we
can still laugh, if somewhat painfully, at youth's aptness at
learning nothing at all, old or new. Of course it is a cliché
that human nature does not change, but it is one that explains why the poem can still provide an amusing hour.

Part One, the adventures of Tom Brainless, is probably the
best section of the poem. The youthful Trumbull knew the
college and the students he was talking about, and his satire
is apt and fitting. The student who arrives with glowing letters of recommendation, only to prove a lazy dunce, is hardly
unknown today. The college curriculum, whose staid con-
servatism so bothered the young Trumbull, has changed in its
content if not in its character, but that does not lessen Trumbull's wit at its expense. And any teacher today will smile at
the conclusion of Tom's school teaching experience:

> The year is done; he takes his leave;
> The children smile; the parents grieve;
> And seek again, their school to keep,
> One just as good, and just as cheap.

Turning Tom into a dunce in the clergy, "As thieves of old,
t' avoid the halter,/ Took refuge in the holy altar," does not

perhaps strike us as quite so funny—as apparently it did not a number of Trumbull's contemporaries—but it was not intended to. A satirist without some edge to his wit is hardly a satirist at all. And so Part One goes, sometimes an attack on the dullard that Tom represents, and sometimes an attack on the foibles of the institutions that shelter him. With the abandon of a young satirist, Trumbull strikes out at whatever seems to need correction or chastisement, and thoroughly enjoys himself while doing it.

Parts Two and Three, the careers of Dick Hairbrain, the country fop and man about town, and of Harriet Simper, the silly young coquette, do not quite come up to the same standard. Perhaps Trumbull had been frightened at the abuse he apparently received from those who read personal references into Part One or who thought it simply an attack on the college or the clergy. Or perhaps in reaching out beyond his own experience toward the stock figures of English satire he exceeded his maturity or his observation. Whatever the reason, the satire of the last two parts is milder and the immediacy is less. But they still have amusement to offer and an occasional sting that may be felt yet. In one respect both parts are a direct continuation of Part One and carry on something of its effectiveness, for both are equally concerned with the problems and the failures of education. Education, in fact, may be called the central theme of the poem as a whole: Tom is the satiric example of the dullard in school; Dick, the wastrel and the careless; Harriet, the silly and the misguided. And the system through which they are put is little better: the college of Tom and Dick offers no intellectual immediacy or excitement, devoting itself to the learned and the stuffy, and Harriet's schooling shows the failure of the popular view of education for women:

> And why should girls be learn'd or wise?
> Books only serve to spoil their eyes.
> The studious eye but faintly twinkles,
> And reading paves the way to wrinkles.

In an America today so exercised over the shortcomings of

its education, the poem seems particularly alive. Parts Two
and Three have their other pleasures too, of course, for we
can still enjoy the glance at the young man and the pretty
miss out to charm the world and make it their private dish.
If they do not emerge as very believable characters, or if their
progress reminds us of the many other "progresses" of the
century—even the much harsher ones of a Hogarth—it
doesn't make much difference, for the effect of the satire
remains, and the many surface details of scene and clothing,
gossip and manners are there to charm and amuse us.

Something of Trumbull's satiric intentions—as well as the
popular effect of his satire—appears in the biting prefaces to
the three parts. Trumbull dropped the preface to the second
part in the 1820 edition, and subsequent editions have not
generally reprinted even those to the first and third parts. It
is too bad, for some of the human interest of the poem is in
them. In the preface to Part One Trumbull carefully points
out his intention to attack the errors of the colleges and also
the laxity of the clergy in its failure to exclude the ignorant
and irreligious, all in hopes that he can contribute to im-
provement. But the preface to Part Two shows that the public had failed to understand what he was doing. Almost
inevitably, Part One had been read by some as simply an
attack on the college and the clergy; and Trumbull roars
back in counterattack against "the Envious and Malicious
Reader." Most later commentators seem to take his words at
their face value and to see Trumbull as an embittered man
striking back at his enemies. Of course there is some bitter-
ness, but it is difficult to read the preface with all that solem-
nity and seriousness; the last paragraph alone—offering the
preface to anyone who wants to deserve it—would seem
enough to indicate that Trumbull is enjoying himself too and
means the preface in its own way to be as comic as the poem
itself, comedy founded on satire. Whatever the exact intention, the preface does have a bite that is still effective—apparently too strong a bite for the older and more staid John
Trumbull when he came back to it. Yet there must have been
something to his sensitivity to criticism, for the preface to

Part Three is much more restrained and very careful to point out exactly what he is doing in the poem to follow: he is not attacking womanhood itself but the neglect of women's education that leads to the foibles that men find. One wonders whether the women accepted such careful distinctions. Trumbull, in fact, keeps protesting his virtuous intentions so explicitly that the modern reader would like to protest himself. But even in enforced mildness, Trumbull is not entirely tamed and manages—perhaps in a forgetful moment—to get in a word about being "ignorantly or wilfully misunderstood." John Trumbull may have had his feelings, but there is no question that he was human.

By the time of the publication of *M'Fingal,* he had become more judicious. Or perhaps he is equally personal and immediate but has simply chosen the popular position so that he has the protection of the impersonality of political warfare and nationalistic sentiment. All right thinking citizens had to agree with him, and his attacks no longer seemed private spite or radical opinion but the patriotic and spirited efforts of a good American. After the first canto appeared in 1776, friends even urged him to continue it as a patriotic duty and a valuable contribution to the national spirit in the war. The completed version of 1782 appeared in time to catch the new American nationalism in its first full growth, and the poem continued to hold patriotic approval for the next century. It is no surprise to find the poem, despite its length, Trumbull's most popular work from the time of its first publication to the present. Even before its final version in the collected works of 1820, it went through twenty-three editions, not counting a number of pirated editions. An illustrated edition of 1795, apparently one of the reprints published with Trumbull's express consent, points to the sort of popular reading that it was receiving. And as an indication of its acceptance among professional men of letters, an edition of 1799 now in the Humanities Research Center of the University of Texas may be pointed out. On the back of the title page Joseph Dennie (1768–1812), the popular essayist, editor, man-about-letters of the day, has written: "John Trumbull Esq. is the author of this poem. which in copious wit, is second only to the cantos of Butler & in vigor, dignity & greatness is superior even to the 'surpassing worth of Sr. Hudibras.' When the Politics of McFingall are forgotten, when the name of whig becomes obsolete, & Anglo Americans & Englishmen wonder at antient animosity, this poem will be read, respected & admired by every lover of the Jocund muse." Trumbull at last had found public approval of his satire, at the expense perhaps of something of his own interest and private concerns.

M'Fingal takes the proper stand certainly and lambastes the Tories and the English with the necessary vigor. When the Scotch Tory M'Fingal speaks for his party he succeeds only in making a fool of himself and in bringing laughter down on the Tory position—and laughter, as Trumbull had discovered, was a powerful and frightening weapon. On closer reading, however, particularly at a safe distance from the high feelings of the day, the weapon is not aimed entirely at the Tories. Often M'Fingal's attacks on the patriotic Whigs have a sting that M'Fingal's own ludicrousness cannot soothe or lessen. In the third canto, for instance, lines 41–108 have enough validity to make them difficult to dismiss even for the staunch patriot. A few of the lines will demonstrate the tone:

> For Liberty in your own by-sense
> Is but for crimes a patent licence;
> To break of law th' Egyptian yoke,
> And throw the world in common stock,
> Reduce all grievances and ills
> To Magna Charta of your wills,
> Establish cheats and frauds and nonsense,
> Fram'd by the model of your conscience.

Trumbull was a moderate, and a lawyer too, and could not bring himself to accept the violent fanaticism of the day that took from even an enemy his traditional and legal rights and denied the whole concept of deliberation and due means. Liberty poles, tar and feathers, and lynchings, even when on the right political side, were hardly what Trumbull was supporting, and even while he jeers at the Tories he takes care to glance acidly at the super patriots who would take the law into their own hands. He has other reservations about the patriots too—particularly when they are as dull and as long-winded as the Tories—but the careful reader will discover them for himself. It is enough to say that even in a time of high emotion Trumbull retained the objective, even disinterested, eye of the true satirist, and hit out at what he believed needed chastisement. The occasion and the subject of his comic satire had changed but the satire itself had not. Unlike his earlier work, however, *M'Fingal* provoked no public indignation; the explanation is probably simply that we enjoy seeing the other fellow attacked, and in the pleasure are likely not to recognize ourselves, at least for the moment.

Trumbull seems never to have been a flaming patriot anyway; his nature, his education, even his family inheritance were all against it. At best perhaps he should be called a literary patriot, for his interests in large part even in *M'Fingal* are literary interests. The poem itself suggests its familiar literary background, and if there were any doubt, Trumbull's letter to the Marquis de Chastellux discussing the poem, later printed in the 1820 edition, would point out his deliberately "literary" intention. The rough verse with its comic hudibrastic rhymes echoes Butler, of course, and often points to Trumbull's familiarity with the verse of Charles Churchill and Swift and Pope and other satiric poets of the century. In particular the poem illustrates Trumbull's familiarity with the conventions of the mock heroic, or "high burlesque" as he calls it in his letter to the marquis, the humorous parody of the conventions of the heroic epic of the sort most familiar today in such greater works of the time as Dryden's *Mac-Flecknoe* or Pope's *Rape of the Lock*. Canto Three in particular illustrates the technique when M'Fingal's single combat and heroic defeat are described as they might have been by one of the great epic poets in a moment of drunken comedy. To avoid any possible failure to recognize the parody, Trumbull in a note to line 262 even points out the

similarity to Homer, Virgil and Milton, and later in the verse
itself makes his point after a mock epic simile:

> The deadly spade discharg'd a blow
> Tremendous on his rear below:
> His bent knee fail'd, and void of strength,
> Stretch'd on the ground his manly length;
> Like antient oak o'erturn'd he lay,
> Or tow'rs to tempests fall'n a prey,
> And more things else—but all men know 'em,
> If slightly vers'd in Epic Poem.   (421–28)

The poem is full too of "low" burlesque literary allusions,
either particular or general; not only heroic verse but the
other all but sacred—and even the sacred—classics are given
their share of comic use, sometimes in apparent parody of
the scholarly tendency of the day to make all points by classical or Biblical reference, sometimes in the simple fun of
burlesque, sometimes just because Trumbull could assume
that his readers would see the comic point buried in the reference. To read the poem with full enjoyment, one ought now
to be as steeped in the traditions of literature as Trumbull
himself was.

And yet it is not necessary for the reader to recognize all
of the literary references or even to know a great deal about
the literary traditions in order to enjoy the poem. The prob-
lem is similar to that posed by the many references to historical details of the revolutionary period: if they are recognized,
fine; if not, the greater part of the enjoyment of the poem still
remains. And after all, for those who want to go into the
details, the notes are always there at the end of this edition.
The general political situation must be understood, of course,
and the general literary aim of the poem, but beyond that no
special knowledge is necessary. For the true pleasure of the
poem for most modern readers is not, or at least not entirely,
in its historical interest but in its general display of wit and
humor for a satiric end. If it were not for the satiric wit, in
fact, the poem would be a little disappointing. It is not great
poetry and does not pretend to be; Trumbull too often lets

his comic purpose override even his poetic sensitivities. As comic verse it does occasionally rise to fine passages of real poetic wit such as the characterization of "Gentleman Johnny":

> Behold that martial Macaroni,
> Compound of Phoebus and Bellona,
> With warlike sword and singsong lay,
> Equipp'd alike for feast or fray,
> Where equal wit and valour join;
> This, this is he, the famed Burgoyne. (IV, 34–38)

But the passages are not generally long sustained, and the reader must too often content himself in long sections with a few memorable couplets:

> True to their King, with firm devotion,
> For conscience sake and hop'd promotion. (IV, 851–2)

It seems fair to say too that the poem is too long; Trumbull might better have left the debates in town meeting of the first and second cantos condensed into one canto, as it was in the original printing, and might have foreshortened even more the detailed panorama of the war offered by M'Fingal's second sight in the fourth canto. Then too, the characterization is weak; M'Fingal is seldom more than a disembodied comic voice, and his Whig opponent of the first two cantos, Honorius, is so clearly and so dully a trumpet for the proper sentiments that it is difficult even to remember his name. Only those real, historical persons attacked—Gage, Howe, Loring, Hutchinson, and the like—have a life of their own, and that is the life of caricature.

If one is willing to read simply for the amusement that the poem has to offer, however, he will not be disappointed. For Trumbull's satiric wit is there in profusion, even if the occasion and the structure of the poem, even the character of the speakers, exist only to offer an opportunity for the wit. The best advice would seem to be to relax and enjoy it, just as it would be enjoyable today to read a wit with a fine sense of the ludicrous commenting on our own wars and politics, our great rumbling national actions and our petty local tempests, our national saints and our devils, our friends and our enemies. The American revolution now seems far back in time, but Trumbull with his timeless sense of the comic makes us see that people then were not so much different from people now, and that human wit can live even when the occasion that called it forth has long since disappeared. In this sense of living on past its own time and occasion *M'Fingal* is like *The Progress of Dulness*. Both poems amuse by reminding us in a witty fashion of the foibles and the foolishness of the human being, and both astonish us a little—in a provincial pride that would have delighted John Trumbull—that even the eighteenth century still has a great deal to say to the twentieth.

A NOTE ON THE TEXT

THE FINAL REVISED VERSION OF TRUMBULL'S POEMS APPEARS in *The Poetical Works of John Trumbull, LL.D.*, two volumes, Hartford, 1820. This text might seem the proper one to reprint, and most later editions have reprinted it. But *The Progress of Dulness* was completed in 1773, and the first canto of *M'Fingal* in 1775, leaving some forty-five years between the first versions and the last. During that long period the literary demands and tastes of the new country changed almost as much as its political position. Since Trumbull's satires are so firmly locked to their own times, it does not seem desirable to reprint a text that represents even to a small extent the visions and revisions of a different age. The text here is, for the first time, an accurate reproduction of the first complete edition of each poem, with all of the idiosyncrasies of colonial spelling and punctuation. The title pages alone are slightly altered for the sake of appearance.

The text of *The Progress of Dulness* is that of the first edition [New Haven, Conn.]: Part One in 1772, and Parts Two and Three in 1773. Part One was also issued in a revised second edition in 1773: Trumbull corrected misprints, restored two couplets that had been omitted in printing (or at least that is a reasonable assumption, since both appear at the point of division between pages in the original edition), and made a few changes in punctuation as well as some half-dozen small stylistic changes in wording. Except for these few changes, there are no important differences in the two editions. And unfortunately, the second edition has its own share of printer's errors. For the sake of consistency then, the text reproduced here—for the first time—is that of the first edition, with some silent correction of errors, inconsistencies and possibly confusing punctuation, as authorized by the second edition.

For the benefit of the scholar interested in absolute textual purity, the following changes from the text of the first edition of Part One are made in conformity with the second edition:

Preface : comma substituted for semicolon after *mathematics*.

: letter *a* added to *reserches* (*researches*).

: *hath* changed to *have* in the last sentence.

line   43 : letter *g* added to *teasin*, followed by added comma (*teasing*).

50 : *Tulley* changed to *Tully*.

58 : semicolon added at end of line.

62 : period substituted for colon at end of line.

78 : semicolon substituted for comma at end of line.

116 : comma added at end of line.

117 : apostrophe added to *justice* (*justice'*).

151 : *Tulley* changed to *Tully*.

156 : comma deleted after *rhymes*.

212 : semicolon substituted for comma at end of line.

244 : footnote: period added at end.

264 : semicolon substituted for comma at end of line.

281 : indentation for new verse paragraph added.

304 : period substituted for comma at end of line.

317–18 : couplet added.

330 : colon substituted for semicolon at end of line.

377 : apostrophe added to *deists* (*deist's*).

379 : comma added after *wish*.

427–28 : couplet added.

448 : comma substituted for period at end of line.

In Part Two, there are four minor editorial changes:

line 37 : period deleted at end of line.

331 : comma substituted for period at end of line.

376 : *scenes* substituted for *seenes*.

399 : comma deleted at end of line; comma added after *unaw'd*.

In Part Three, there are six silent changes in conformity with the errata slip issued with the poem. In addition, there are three editorial corrections:

line 343 : comma substituted for period at end of line.

563 : apostrophe omitted in *Lawyer's* (*Lawyers*).

665 : *forth* changed to *for th'*.

What were to be the first two cantos of *M'Fingal* in the complete version were published in 1776 (dated 1775 on the titlepage) as Canto One. In 1782 Trumbull completed the poem, divided the original Canto One into two cantos, and published the poem in four cantos printed together. To make the division, it was necessary to add a number of lines at the end of the first canto and the beginning of the second, and Trumbull took the opportunity also to add a few lines here and there throughout the cantos and generally to make small revisions and corrections where they seemed needed. It is this version of 1782, published by Hudson and Goodwin in Hartford, that is printed here. For absolute consistency perhaps the text of 1775 should have been chosen for the first half, but that seems entirely too pedantic. The parts of the poem must fit together as a whole, and the text of 1782 is the first version of the poem as a complete unit. At any rate, the difference in time between the first partial appearance and the final completed poem is reasonably small.

The poem is so well printed in the original edition that except for a few small printer's errors no corrections in the text are necessary, despite the occasional vagaries of spelling and punctuation that may or may not belong to the printing shop. Only these errors have been corrected:

Canto One, line 50: period added at end of line.

Canto One, line 194: period for comma at end.

Canto One, line 501: apostrophe deleted before *gain*.

Canto One, note to line 537: period substituted for comma at end.

Canto Two, line 44: *you* changed to *your*.

Canto Three, line 625: *goal* corrected to *gaol*.

Canto Four, line 188: *traunting* corrected to *truanting*.

Canto Four, line 367: *goal* again corrected to *gaol*.

Canto Four, line 680: quotation mark deleted at end.

The illustrations here are reproduced from early editions of Trumbull in the Humanities Research Center of the University of Texas: the dust jacket from the *Poetical Works* of 1820 and the others from the first illustrated edition, published in New York in 1795. The Research Center also provided good copies of the rare Part Two of *The Progress of Dulness* and the 1782 first edition of *M'Fingal*, as well as later editions of both, for the necessary textual checking and for occasional help with the notes. The American Literature Collection of the Yale University Library very kindly allowed photostats of its complete *Progress of Dulness* for further checks. My thanks go to both. To be very sure that variants do not appear in these editions, I have also compared various copies in the Library of Congress, The Columbia University Library, the New York Public Library, and those offered in microprint by the American Antiquarian Society's series of reproductions, "Early American Imprints 1639–1800."

My further thanks go to the Excellence Fund and the University Research Institute of the University of Texas for financial help in preparing this edition. The scholar today is dependent on such funds and should praise their silent help wherever possible. John Trumbull would undoubtedly approve, although perhaps with a sardonic reservation or two, as he sees them "with lib'ral hand,/ Spread useful learning o'er the land."

THE PROGRESS

OF DULNESS

THE PROGRESS OF DULNESS

PART FIRST

or

The
Rare Adventures
of
Tom Brainless

SHEWING: What his Father and Mother said of him—how he went to College, and what he learned there—how he took his Degree, and went to keeping school—how afterwards he became a great man and wore a wig—and how any body else may do the same.—The like never before published.

Daries, daries, astataries, dissunapiter: huat, hanat,
ista, pista, fista, domi abo, damnostra.
Carmen antiquum contra luxata membra.

Very proper to be kept in all Families.

AUTHOR'S
PREFACE

"Pray what does the author mean?" is the first question most readers will ask, and the last they are able to answer. Therefore in a word I will explain the subject and design of the following poem.

The subject is the state of the times in regard to literature and religion. The author was prompted to write by a hope that it might be of use to point out, in a clear, concise, and striking manner, those general errors, that hinder the advantages of education, and the growth of piety. The subject is inexhaustible; nor is my design yet completed. This first part describes the principal mistakes in one course of life, and exemplifies the following well-known truth, That to the frequent scandal, as well of religion, as learning, a fellow, without any share of genius, or application to study, may pass with credit through life, receive the honors of a liberal education, and be admitted to the right hand of fellowship

*among ministers of the gospel. That, except in one neigh-
bouring province, nonsense and ignorance wander unmolested at our colleges, examinations are dwindled to meer
form and ceremony, and after four years dozing there, no
one is ever refused the honors of a degree, on account of
dulness and insufficiency. That the* meer *knowledge of
antient languages, of the abstruser parts of mathematics, and
the dark researches of metaphysics, is of little advantage in
any business or profession in life. That it would be more
beneficial, in every place of public education, to take pains
in teaching the elements of oratory, the grammar of the
English tongue, and the elegancies of style, and composition.
That in numberless instances throughout these colonies, sufficient care hath not been taken to exclude the ignorant and
irreligious, from the sacred desk. That this tenderness to the
undeserving, tends to debase the dignity of the clergy, and
to hinder many worthy men from undertaking the office
of the ministry. And that the virulent controversies of the
present day, concerning religious, or in many cases, meerly
speculative opinions, savouring so highly of vanity and osten-
tation, and breathing a spirit so opposite to christian benevolence, have done more hurt to the cause of religion, than all
the malice, the ridicule, and the folly of its enemies.*

The

Rare Adventures

of

Tom Brainless

"OUR *Tom* is grown a sturdy boy;
His progress fills my heart with joy;
A steady soul that yields to rule,
And quite ingenious too at school.
Our master says, (I'm sure he's right)
There's not a lad in town so bright.
He'll cypher bravely, write and read,
And say his catechism and creed,
And scorns to hesitate or faulter
In primmer, spelling-book or psalter.   *10*
Hard work indeed—he does not love it;
His genius is too much above it.
Give him a good substantial teacher,
I'll lay he makes a special preacher.
I've lov'd good learning all my life:
We'll send the lad to college, wife."

Thus sway'd by fond and sightless passion,
His parents hold a consultation:
If on their couch, or round their fire,
I need not tell, or you enquire.   *20*
    The point's agreed; the boy well pleas'd,
From country cares and labours eas'd;
No more to rise by break of day
To drive home cows, or deal out hay;
To work no more in snow and hail,
And blow his fingers o'er the flail,
Or mid the toils of harvest sweat
Beneath the summer's sultry heat.
Serene, he bids the farm good-bye,
And quits the plow without a sigh.   *30*
Propitious to their constant friend,
The pow'rs of idleness attend.
    So to the priest in form he goes,
Prepar'd to study and to doze.
The parson in his youth before,
Had run the same dull progress o'er:
His sole concern to see with care
His church, and farm in good repair.
His skill in tongues, that once he knew,
Had bid him long, a last adieu;   *40*
Away his latin rules had fled,
And Greek had vanish'd from his head.
    Then view our youth with grammar teazing,
Untaught in meaning, sense or reason;
Of knowledge e'er he gain his fill, he
Must diet long on husks of *Lillie,*
Drudge on for weary months in vain;
By mem'ry's strength, and dint of brain;
From thence to murd'ring *Virgil's* verse,
And construing *Tully,* into farce,   *50*
Or lab'ring with his grave preceptor,

In Greek to blunder o'er a chapter.
The latin testament affords
The needy help, and ready words;
At hand the dictionary laid,
Gives up it's page in frequent aid;
Hard by the lexicon and grammar,
Those helps for mem'ry when they stammer;
The lesson's short; the priest contented;
His task to hear is sooner ended.   60
He lets him mind his own concerns,
Then tells his parents how he learns.
      A year thus spent in gathering knowledge,
The lad sets forth t' unlade at college,
While down his sire and priest attend him,
To introduce and recommend him:
Or if detain'd, a letter's sent
Of much apocryphal content,
To set him forth, (how dull soever)
As very learn'd and very clever;   70
A genius of the first emission,
With burning love for erudition;
So studious he'll outwatch the moon
And think the planets set too soon;
He had but little time to fit in;
Examination too must frighten;
Depend upon't he must do well,
He knows much more than he can tell;
Admit him, and in little space
He'll beat his rivals in the race;   80
His father's incomes are but small,
He comes now, if he comes at all.
      So said, so done, at college now
He enters well—no matter how—
New scenes awhile his fancy please,
But all must yield to love of ease.

In the same round condemn'd each day,
To study, read, recite and pray;
To make his hours of business double—
He can't endure th' increasing trouble: *90*
And finds at length, as times grow pressing,
All plagues are easier than his lesson.
With sleepy eyes and count'nance heavy,
With much excuse of *non paravi,
Much absence, tardes* and *egresses,*
The college-evil on him siezes.
Then ev'ry book, which ought to please,
Stirs up the seeds of dire disease:
Greek spoils his eyes (the print's so fine)
Grown dim with study—and with wine;   *100*
Of *Tully's* latin much afraid,
Each page, he calls the doctor's aid;
While geometry, with lines so crooked,
Sprains all his wits to overlook it.
His sickness puts on every name,
It's cause and uses still the same;
'Tis tooth-ach, cholic, gout or stone,
With phases various as the moon:
But though through all the body spread,
Still makes its cap'tal seat, the head.   *110*
In all diseases, 'tis expected,
The weakest parts be most infected.
   Kind headach hail! thou blest disease,
The friend of idleness and ease;
Who mid the still and dreary bound,
Where college-walls her sons surround,
In spite of fears, in justice' spight,
Assum'st o'er laws dispensing right,
Set'st from his talk the blunderer free,

* *Non paravi,* I have not prepared for recitation. An excuse commonly given.

Excus'd by dulness and by thee.   *120*
Thy vot'ries bid a bold defiance
To all the calls and threats of science,
Slight learning human and divine,
And hear no prayers, and fear no fine.
  And yet how oft the studious gain,
The dulness of a letter'd brain;
Despising such low things the while
As English grammar, phrase and style;
Despising ev'ry nicer art,
That aids the tongue, or mends the heart: *130*
Read antient authors o'er in vain,
Nor taste one beauty they contain;
Humbly on trust accept the sense,
But deal for words at vast expence;
Search well how ev'ry term must vary
From lexicon to dictionary;
And plodding on in one dull tone,
Gain antient tongues, and lose their own,
Bid every graceful charm defiance,
And woo the skeleton of science.   *140*
  Come ye who finer arts despise,
And scoff at verse as heathen lies;
In all the pride of dulness rage
At *Pope,* or *Milton's* deathless page;
Or stung by truth's deep-searching line,
Rave ev'n at rhymes as low as mine:
Say ye who boast the name of wise,
Wherein substantial learning lies.
Is it, superb in classic lore,
To speak what *Homer* spoke before,   *150*
To write the language *Tully* wrote,
The style, the cadence and the note?
Is there a charm in sounds of Greek,
No language else can learn to speak;

That cures distemper'd brains at once,
Like *Pliny's* rhymes for broken bones?
Is there a spirit found in latin,
That must evap'rate in translating?
And say, are sense and genius bound
To any vehicles of sound?   *160*
   Is it by mathematic's aid
To count the worlds in light array'd,
To know each star, that lights it's eye,
To sparkle in the midnight sky?
Say ye, who draw the curious line
Between the useful and the fine,
How little can this noble art
It's aid in human things impart,
Or give to life a chearful ray,
And force our pains, and cares away.   *170*
   Is it to know whate'er was done
Above the circle of the sun?
Is it to lift the active mind
Beyond the bounds by heav'n design'd;
And leave our little world at home,
Through realms of entity to roam;
Attempt the secrets dark to scan,
Eternal wisdom hid from man;
For sense, deal loads of definitions,
And fritter truth in sub-divisions,   *180*
And make religion but the sign
In din of battle when to join?
Vain man, to madness still a prey,
Thy space a point, thy life a day,
A feeble worm, that aim'st to stride
In all the foppery of pride!
The glimmering lamp of reason's ray
Was giv'n to guide thy darksome way.
Why wilt thou spread thine insect-wings,

And strive to reach sublimer things?   *190*
Thy doubts confess, thy blindness own,
Nor vex thy thoughts with scenes unknown.
Indulgent heav'n to man below,
Hath all explain'd we need to know;
Hath clearly taught enough to prove
Content below, and bliss above.
Thy boastful wish how proud and vain,
While heav'n forbids the vaunting strain!
For metaphysics rightly shown
But teach how little can be known: *200*
Though quibbles still maintain their station,
Conjecture serves for demonstration,
Armies of pens drawn forth to fight,
And ******* and ****** write.
   Oh! might I live to see that day,
When sense shall point to youths their way;
Through every maze of science guide;
O'er education's laws preside;
The good retain; with just discerning
Explode the fopperies of learning;   *210*
Give antient arts their real due,
Explain their faults, and beauties too;
Teach where to imitate, and mend,
And point their uses and their end.
Then bright philosophy would shine,
And ethics teach the laws divine;
Our youths might reach each nobler art,
That shews a passage to the heart;
From antient languages well known
Transfuse new beauties to our own;   *220*
With taste and fancy well refin'd,
Where moral rapture warms the mind,
From schools dismiss'd, with lib'ral hand,
Spread useful learning o'er the land;

And bid the eastern world admire
Our rising worth, and bright'ning fire.
    But while through fancy's realms we roam,
The main concern is left at home;
Return'd, our hero still we find
The same, as blundering and as blind.   *230*
    Four years at college doz'd away
In sleep, and slothfulness and play,
Too dull for vice, with clearest conscience,
Charg'd with no fault, but that of nonsense,
(And nonsense long, with serious air
Has wander'd unmolested there)
He passes trial fair, and free,
And takes in form his first degree.
    A scholar see him now commence
Without the aid of books or sense: *240*
For passing college cures the brain,
Like mills to grind men young again.
The scholar-dress, that once array'd him,
The charm, *Admitto te ad gradum,
With touch of parchment can refine,
And make the veriest coxcomb shine,
Confer the gift of tongues at once,
And fill with sense the vacant dunce.
So kingly crowns contain quintessence
Of worship, dignity and presence;   *250*
Give learning, genius, virtue, worth,
Wit, valor, wisdom and so forth;
Hide the bald pate, and cover o'er
The cap of folly worn before.
    Our hero's wit and learning now may
Be prov'd by token of *Diploma,*
Of that *Diploma,* which with speed

* *Admitto te ad gradum,* I admit you to a degree; part of the words
used in conferring the honors of college.

He learns to construe and to read;
And stalks abroad with conscious stride,
In all the airs of pedant-pride,   260
With passport sign'd for wit and knowledge,
And current under seal of college.
    Few months now past, he sees with pain
His purse as empty as his brain;
His father leaves him then to fate,
And throws him off, as useless weight;
But gives him good advice, to teach
A school at first, and then to preach.
    Thou reason'st well; it must be so;
For nothing else thy son can do.   270
As thieves of old, t' avoid the halter,
Took refuge in the holy altar:
Oft dulness flying from disgrace
Finds safety in that sacred place;
There boldly rears his head, or rests
Secure from ridicule or jests;
Where dreaded satire may not dare
Offend his wig's extremest hair;
Where scripture sanctifies his strains,
And rev'rence hides the want of brains.   280
    Next see our youth at school appear,
Procur'd for forty pounds a year,
His ragged regiment round assemble,
Taught, not to read, but fear and tremble.
Before him, rods prepare his way,
Those dreaded antidotes to play.
Then thron'd aloft in elbow-chair,
With solemn face and awful air,
He tries with ease and unconcern,
To teach what ne'er himself could learn;   290
Gives law and punishment alone,
Judge, jury, bailiff, all in one;

Holds all good learning must depend
Upon his rod's extremest end,
Whose great electric virtue's such,
Each genius brightens at the touch;
With threats and blows (incitements pressing)
Drives on his lads to learn each lesson;
Thinks flogging cures all moral ills,
And breaks their heads to break their wills.   *300*
    The year is done; he takes his leave;
The children smile; the parents grieve;
And seek again, their school to keep,
One just as good, and just as cheap.
    Now to some priest, that's fam'd for teaching,
He goes to learn the art of preaching;
And settles down with earnest zeal
Sermons to study, and to steal:
Six months from all the world retires
To kindle up his cover'd fires;   *310*
Learns the nice art, to make with ease
The scriptures speak whate'er he please;
With judgment unperceiv'd to quote
What *Poole* explain'd, or *Henry* wrote;
To give the gospel new editions,
Split doctrines into propositions,
Draw motives, uses, inferences,
And torture words in thousand senses;
Learn the grave style and goodly phrase,
Safe-handed down from *Cromwell's* days,   *320*
And shun with anxious care, the while
Th' infection of a modern style:
Or on the wings of folly fly
Aloft in metaphysic sky;
The system of the world explain,
Till night and chaos come again;
Deride what old divines can say,

Point out to heav'n a nearer way:
Explode all known, establish'd rules,
Affirm our fathers all were fools: *330*
The present age is growing wise,
But wisdom in her cradle lies;
Late, like *Minerva,* born and bred;
Not from a *Joves's,* but scribler's head,
While thousand youths their homage lend her,
And nursing fathers rock and tend her.
   Round him much manuscript is spread,
Extracts from living works, and dead,
Themes, sermons, plans of controversy,
That hack and mangle without mercy,   *340*
And whence, to glad the reader's eyes,
The future dialogue shall rise.
   At length matur'd the grand design,
He stalks abroad, a grave divine.
   Mean while, from ev'ry distant seat
At stated time the clergy meet.
Our hero comes, his sermon reads,
Explains the doctrine of his creeds,
A licence gains to preach and pray,
And makes his bow, and goes his way.   *350*
   What though his wits could ne'er dispense
One page of grammar, or of sense;
What though his learning be so slight,
He scarcely knows to spell or write;
What though his skull be cudgel-proof!
He's orthodox, and that's enough.
   Perhaps with genius we'd dispense;
But sure we look at least for sense.
   Ye fathers of our Church, attend
The serious counsels of a friend,   *360*
Whose utmost wish, in nobler ways,
Your sacred dignity to raise.

Though blunt the style, the truths set down
Ye can't deny—though some may frown.
   Yes, there are men, nor those a few,
The foes of virtue, and of you;
Who, nurtur'd long in dulness' school,
Make vice their trade, and sin by rule,
Who deem it courage, heav'n to brave,
And wit, to scoff at all that's grave;   *370*
Vent stolen jests, with strange grimaces,
From folly's book of common places:
While mid the simple throng around
Each kindred blockhead greets the sound,
And, like electric fire, at once,
The laugh is caught from dunce to dunce.
   The deist's scoffs ye may despise;
Within yourselves your danger lies;
For who would wish, neglecting rule,
To aid the triumphs of a fool?   *380*
From heav'n at first your order came,
From heav'n receiv'd it's sacred name,
Indulg'd to man, to point the way,
That leads from darkness up to day.
Your highborn dignity attend,
And view your origin and end.
   While human souls are all your care,
By warnings, counsels, preaching, prayer,
In bands of christian friendship join'd,
Where pure affection warms the mind,   *390*
While each performs the pious race,
Nor dulness e'er usurps a place;
No vice shall brave your awful test,
Nor folly dare to broach the jest,
Each waiting eye shall humbly bend,
And rev'rence on your steps attend.
   But when each point of serious weight,

Is torn with wrangling and debate,
When truth, mid rage of dire divisions,
Is left, to fight for definitions,   *400*
And fools assume your sacred place,
It threats your order with disgrace;
Bids genius from your seats withdraw,
And seek the pert, loquacious law;
Or deign in physic's paths to rank,
With ev'ry quack and mountebank;
Or in the ways of trade content,
Plod ledgers o'er of cent. per cent.
   While in your seats so sacred, whence
We look for piety and sense,   *410*
Pert dulness raves in schoolboy style;
Your friends must blush, your foes will smile.
While men, who teach the glorious way,
Where heav'n unfolds celestial day,
Assume the talk sublime, to bring
The message of th' eternal king,
Disgrace those honors they receive,
And want that sense, they aim to give.
   Now in the desk with solemn air,
Our hero makes his audience stare;   *420*
Asserts with all dogmatic boldness,
Where impudence is yok'd to dulness;
Reads o'er his notes with halting pace,
Mask'd in the stiffness of his face;
With gestures such as might become
Those statues once that spoke at *Rome,*
Or *Livy's* ox, that to the state
Declar'd the oracles of fate,
In awkward tones, nor said, nor sung,
Slow-rumbling o'er the faltring tongue,   *430*
Two hours his drawling speech holds on,
And names it preaching when he's done.

With roving tir'd, he fixes down
For life, in some unsettled town.
People and priest full well agree;
For why—they know no more than he.
Vast tracts of unknown lands he gains,
Better than those the moon contains:
There deals in preaching and in prayer,
And starves on sixty pounds a year,   *440*
And culls his texts, and tills his farm,
And does no good, and little harm;
On sunday in his best array,
Deals forth the dulness of the day;
And while above he spends his breath,
The yawning audience nod beneath.
    Thus glib-tongu'd *Merc'ry* in his hand
Stretch'd forth the sleep-compelling wand,
Each eye in endless doze to keep—
The God of speaking, and of sleep.   *450*

PART SECOND

or

An Essay on
The Life and Character of
Dick Hairbrain

OF FINICAL MEMORY

Being an Astronomical Calendar,
Calculated for the Meridian of New-York,
North Latitude, 41°. West Longitude, 72°:30′
but which may serve without material Error, for any
of the neighbouring Climates:

CONTAINING : Among other curious and surprizing Particulars,
Dick's Soliloquy on a College-Life—a Description of a Country-
Fop—Receipt to make a Gentleman, with the Fop's Creed and
Exposition of the Scriptures—Dick's gradual Progress from a
Clown to a Coxcomb—His Travels, Gallantry, and Opinion of
the Ladies—His *Peripaetia* and *Catastrophe*, with the Moral
and Application of the whole.

Published for the universal Benefit of Mankind

AUTHOR'S
PREFACE

It is become an universal custom for every Author, before he gives himself up to the fury of the Critics, to make his dying speech in a Preface; in which, according to the usual style of criminals, he confesses his faults, tells the temptations that led him to the crime of scribbling, gives good advice to the rest of his fraternity, and throws himself upon the mercy of the Court. These speeches are commonly addressed to a sort of imaginary being, called the kind, courteous, candid *and sometimes,* benevolent Reader. *Not that I would deny the existence of such a being, as an Epicurean once did of the soul, because he could not find an account of it, in the complete zoology of animals. The first part of this Poem met with very kind reception from many of this class: nor am I concerned least the second should receive any ill usage from them. Authors have much more to fear from readers of a different stamp; and though we are usually loth to speak out so plainly, the truth is, we should not make such long prologues to the Candid, were we assured of our safety from the attacks of the Malicious. For my own part, being an enemy to ceremony and circumlocution, and having moreover some outstanding accounts to settle, I shall directly address myself to this last kind of Critic; assuring him however, upon my word of honour, that I was not moved to do him this homage, as the Indians are to worship the devil, out of any fear of his power to do mischief; since I have already experienced that his malice has its proper antidote in his impotence.*

TO THE ENVIOUS AND MALICIOUS READER

May it please your Worship, or your Reverence; or your Ill-nature, by what title soever dignified and distinguished:

As you have expressed great resentment against the first part of this Poem and its Author, you might perchance think yourself slighted, if I should let the second come abroad without paying you my proper acknowlegements. I own myself much your debtor; and am only sorry that the number of your brotherhood is so inconsiderable, that the world may perhaps think this dedication almost entirely needless. Had a greater number shown themselves affected, I should have had more grounds to hope that the Poem might be useful. Satire is a medicine very salutary in its effects, but quite unpleasant in its operation; nor do I know a more evident symptom that the potion has taken its proper effect, than the groans and distortions of the Patient.

I had the pleasure, my Illnatured Reader, on the first publication of my poem, to hear the remarks made upon it by a cluster of your fraternity, who might each of them have sate for the picture of Tom Brainless. *And as you may have frequent occasion to talk against it yourself, and yet be at some loss what to alledge in its reproach, I will do you the favor to acquaint you with the result of their criticisms; in order to save you the trouble of so much thinking, and assist you a little in the style and expression of your resentments.*

It was determined by the meeting, nem. con. *that the whole piece was low, paltry stuff, and both scurrilous in the sentiments and dirty in the style; that it was evident, the Author knew nothing of language, or versification, and was incapable of writing with any degree of elegance; that he was an open reviler of the Clergy, and an enemy to truth and learning; that his apparent design was to ridicule religion, disgrace morality, sneer at the present methods of education, and in short, write a satire upon* Yale-College *and the ten commandments; that he treated the subject in the most partial and prejudiced manner, and must certainly be either a Separatist, or a Sandemanian. Though the truth of the assertions in the poem could not so conveniently be denied, yet much was said against the intention of the Author; and it was affirmed that if indeed the world in one or two points was not quite so good, as they could wish it, yet things in the present state could never be altered for the better, and it was folly, or madness alone could propose it.*

Now to give you as much light as possible into this matter, I would assure you, the Author had very little hopes that the world would, in his day, arrive at the point of perfection, from which it is at present he knows not how many leagues distant; and his expectations are not very sanguine, that these pictures of the modern defective manners will do much service. He is fully sensible, that the moral World is as difficult to be moved out of its course, as the natural; that there is in it as much power of resistance or vis inertiae, *as the Philosophers term it; and that the projectors are equally at a loss for engines and foothold. He is as much satisfied that the present year hath borne a sufficient number of fools to keep up the breed, as that there has been a tolerable crop produced every season, for these forty years past. But he*

*thought, though perhaps the picture might not reclaim many,
there could be no harm in trying his hand at the draught:
In which, if the good people, who sate for the painting, have
the ill hap to find themselves drawn with a wide mouth, a
long nose, or a blear eye, he begs of them to get a little ac-
quainted with their own faces, and see whether these be not
their real defects of nature, before they begin to rail at the
Painter, for the badness of their resemblance.*

*I am fully sensible, my Illnatured Reader, that you have
good reasons in your own breast, to account for your resentment against my first essay, and direct you in the manner of
your remarks. You ought in gratitude to defend that careless-
ness in the examination of Candidates for preaching, to
which it is not at all impossible, but you may yourself be
indebted for your reverence and your band. Justly may you
despise the study of those finer Arts and Sciences, of which,
in a smooth journey through life, you never once knew the
want, or perceived the advantages: justly should you under-
value them in comparison with that antient Learning, which
from experience you rightly term* Solid, *as your own wits
were never able to penetrate it. With good reason also do you
affirm the satire to be levelled at the Clergy in general,
since that assertion is the best method of preventing the
public from dragging to view those particular men, at whom
it is, and ought to be, pointed; though you might discern,
with any other eye than that of wilful prejudice, that the
Author hath the highest veneration for the ministerial robe,
or he would never thus trouble himself about the spots that
defile it. As for those,* however dignified in station, *who rail
at the Progress of Dulness, to gain favour with a particular
party, or order of men, he thinks them unworthy the notice
of an answer. He would hint only to such as hope to screen
themselves in the croud, and draw on him the resentment of
those he esteems, by affirming the satire to be general, that
he would thank them, if they would so far throw off the*

mask, that by acquiring a right to their names, he may have an opportunity hereafter to render it more particular. He especially recommends this hint to two Persons, the haughtiest Dullard, and the most impertinent Coxcomb of this age; from whom he has already received numberless favours, and who by their future good conduct may stand a chance, at some fortunate period, to figure at the head of a Dedication to the first and second parts of the Progress of Dulness.

And now, my Evil Reader, with regard to the Poem before you, which is properly a counterpart to the other, I design pretty much to let it speak for itself. Perhaps, since I have now endeavoured to ridicule and explode both extremes, this second part may assist you a little to judge what are the sentiments I would wish to enforce: but in plain truth, I have very little hopes of you. Nevertheless before I leave you, I will tell you one secret, and give you a few words of advice. The secret, which I am sure you would never have been able to discover, is this; In conformity to the delicacy of your taste, I have raised the style of this part, about two degrees by the scale, higher than the other. The advice is, that it will be no unwise proceedure in you to hint that the spirit of the piece is not well supported, nor this part half so good as the first: and an observation, or two, upon the Author's impudence, seasonably introduced, might not be wholly without effect. But as to the old trite way of calling men, Heretics, Deists and Arminians, it hath been lately so much hackneyed and worn out by some Reverend Gentlemen, that I cannot promise it would do you any manner of service.

I cannot conclude without declaring to the world in this public manner, that whoever shall take on himself this character, by criticizing on these Poems in the method above specified, shall have my free licence and permission to appropriate to himself the whole of this dedication, and be distinguished for the future by the title of my Envious and Malicious Reader: and I do assure him that this preface was

*written purposely for him; not designing however to exclude
from a proper share every one, who shall join with him in
those sentiments, from this first day of January, new style,
A.D. 1773, henceforth, and as long as the world shall endure,
be the same term longer or shorter.*

Witness my hand,

THE AUTHOR.

P.S. I Wish you a happy New-year.

The
Life and Character
of
Dick Hairbrain

'TWAS IN A TOWN remote (the place
 We leave the reader wise to guess;
For readers wise can guess full well,
What authors never meant to tell)
There dwelt secure a Country-clown,
The wealthiest Farmer of the town;
Tho' rich by villainy and cheats,
He bought respect by frequent treats;
Gain'd offices by constant seeking,
Squire, Captain, *Deputy* and Deacon;   *10*
Great was his pow'r; his pride as arrant:
One only Son his heir apparent.
He thought the Stripling's parts were quick,
And vow'd to make a man of *Dick;*
Bless'd the pert dunce, and prais'd his looks,
And put him early to his books.

More oaths than words *Dick* learn'd to speak,
And studied knav'ry more than greek;
Three years at school, as usual, spent,
Then all equipt to College went,   20
And pleas'd in prospect, thus bestow'd
His meditations, as he rode.
  "All hail, unvex'd with care and strife,
The bliss of Academic life;
Where kind repose protracts the span,
While Childhood ripens into man;
Where no hard parent's dreaded rage
Curbs the gay sports of youthful age;
Where no vile fear the Genius awes
With grim severity of laws;   30
Where annual troops of Bucks come down,
The flow'r of ev'ry neighb'ring town;
Where wealth and pride and riot wait,
And ev'ry rogue may find his mate.
  Far from those walls, from pleasure's eye,
Let care and grief and labour fly,
The toil to gain the laurel-prize
That dims the anxious student's eyes,
The pedant-air of learned looks,
And long fatigue of turning books.   40
Let poor, dull rogues, with weary pains,
To college come to mend their brains,
And drudge four years, with grave concern,
How they may wiser grow and learn.
Is wealth of indolence afraid,
Or does wit need pedantic aid?
The man of wealth the world decries,
Without the help of learning, wise;
The magic pow'rs of gold, with ease,
Transform us to what shape we please,   50
Give knowledge bright and courage brave,

And wits, that nature never gave.
But nought avails the hoarded treasure;
In spending only lies the pleasure.
    There Vice shall lavish all her charms,
And Rapture fold us in her arms,
Riot shall court the frolic soul,
And Swearing crown the sparkling bowl;
While Wit shall sport with vast applause,
And scorn the feeble tie of laws;   *60*
Our midnight joys no rule shall bound,
While games and dalliance revel round.
Such pleasures youthful years can know,
And Schools there are, that such bestow.
    And oh, that School how greatly blest,
By fate distinguish'd from the rest,
Whose seat is fix'd on sacred ground,
By *Venus'* nunn'ries circled round;
Where not, like monks, in durance hard,
From all the joys of love debarr'd,   *70*
The solitary Youth in pain
For rapture sighs, yet sighs in vain:
But kind occasion prompts desire
And crowns the gay, licentious fire,
And Pleasure courts the sons of Science,
And Whores and Muses hold alliance.
    Not Those *so blest, for ease and sport,
Where Wealth and Idleness resort,
Where free from censure and from shame,
They seek of learning, but the name,   *80*
Their crimes of all degrees and sizes

* "There is a certain Region on the Western Continent, situated within the northern temperate Zone, where in *some* of the most notable and respectable Schools, not only Indolence & Dulness, but almost every Crime, may by the rich be aton'd for with pecuniary satisfaction." *Dudon's Geographical Paradoxes.* No. 45.

Aton'd by golden sacrifices:
Where kind instructors fix their price,
In just degrees on ev'ry vice,
And fierce in zeal 'gainst wicked courses,
Demand repentance—of their purses;
Till sin, thus tax'd, produces clear
A copious income ev'ry year,
And the fair Schools thus free from scruples,
Thrive by the knav'ry of their Pupils.   90
    Ev'n thus the Pope, long since has made
Of human crimes a gainful trade;
Keeps ev'ry pleasing vice for sale,
For cash, by wholesale, or retail.
There, pay the prices and the fees,
Buy rapes, or lies, or what you please,
Then sin secure, with firm reliance,
And bid the ten commands defiance.
    And yet, alas, these happiest Schools
Preserve a set of musty rules,   100
And in their wisest progress show,
Perfection is not found below.
Ev'n there, indulg'd, in humble station,
Learning resides by toleration;
No law forbids the youth to read;
For sense, no tortures are decreed;
There study injures but the name,
And meets no punishment, but shame."
    Thus reas'ning, *Dick* goes forth to find
A College suited to his mind;   110
But bred in distant woods, the Clown
Brings all his country-airs to town;
The odd address with awkward grace,
That bows with all-averted face;
The half heard compliments, whose note
Is swallow'd in the trembling throat;

The stiffen'd gait, the drawling tone,
By which his native place is known;
The blush, that looks, by vast degrees,
Too much like modesty to please: 120
The proud displays of awkward dress,
That all the Country-fop express,
The suit right gay, tho' much belated,
Whose fashion's superannuated;
The watch, depending far in state,
Whose iron chain might form a grate;
The silver buckle, dread to view,
O'ershad'wing all the clumsy shoe;
The white-glov'd hand, that tries to peep
From ruffle, full five inches deep;   130
With fifty odd affairs beside,
The foppishness of country-pride.
   Poor *Dick*! tho' first thy airs provoke
Th' obstrep'rous laugh and scornful joke,
Doom'd all the ridicule to stand,
While each gay dunce shall lend a hand;
Yet let not scorn dismay thy hope
To shine a Witling and a Fop.
Blest impudence the prize shall gain,
And bid thee sigh no more in vain.   140
Thy varied dress shall quickly show
At once the spendthrift and the Beau.
With pert address and noisy tongue,
That scorns the fear of prating wrong,
'Mongst listning coxcombs shalt thou shine,
And ev'ry voice shall echo thine.
As when, disjointed from the stock,
We view with scorn the shapeless block,
The skilful statuary hews us
The wood in any form he chuses;   150
So shall the arts of Fops in town

From thee smooth off the rugged clown,
The rubbish of thy mien shall clear,
Till all the Beau in pomp appear.
   How blest the brainless Fop, whose praise
Is doom'd to grace these happy days,
When wellbred Vice can genius teach,
And fame is placed in Folly's reach;
Impertinence all tastes can hit,
And ev'ry Rascal is a Wit.   *160*
The lowest dunce, without despairing,
May learn the true sublime, of swearing,
Learn the nice art of jests obscene,
(While Ladies wonder what they mean)
The heroism of brazen lungs,
The rhet'ric of eternal tongues;
While whim usurps the name of spirit,
And impudence takes place of merit,
And ev'ry money'd Clown and Dunce
Commences Gentleman at once.   *170*
   For now, by easy rules of trade,
Mechanic Gentlemen are made!
From handycrafts of fashion born;
Those very arts so much their scorn.
To tailors half themselves they owe,
Who makes the clothes, that make the Beau.
   Lo! from the seats, where (Fops to bless)
Learn'd Artists fix the forms of dress,
And sit in consultation grave,
On folded skirt, or straitned sleeve,   *180*
The Coxcomb trips with sprightly haste,
In all the flush of modern taste:
Oft turning, if the day be fair,
To view his shadow's graceful air;
Wellpleas'd with eager eye runs o'er
The laced suit glittring gay before;

The ruffle, where from open'd vest
The rubied brooch adorns the breast;
The coat with length'ning waist behind,
Whose short skirts dangle in the wind;   *190*
The modish hat, whose breadth contains
The measure of its owner's brains;
The stockings gay with silken hues;
The little toe-encircling shoes;
The cane, on whose carv'd top is shown
An head just emblem of his own;
While wrapt in self, with lofty stride,
His little heart elate with pride,
He struts in all the joys of show,
That Tailors give, or Beaus can know.   *200*
    And who for Beauty need repine,
That's sold at ev'ry Barber's sign;
Nor lies in features or complexion,
But curls dispos'd in meet direction,
With strong pomatum's grateful odour,
And *quantum sufficit* of powder?
These charms can shed a sprightly grace,
O'er the dull eye and clumsy face;
While the trim Dancing-master's art
Shall gestures, trips and bows impart,   *210*
Give the gay piece its final touches,
And lend those airs, would lure a Dutchess.
    Thus shines the form, nor aught behind,
The gifts that deck the Coxcomb's mind;
Then hear the daring muse disclose
The sense and Piety of Beaus.
    To grace his speech, let *France* bestow
A set of compliments for show;
Lands of Politeness! that affords
The treasure of newfangled words,   *220*
And endless quantities disburses

Of bows and compliments and curses:
The soft address, with airs so sweet,
That cringes at the Ladies feet;
The pert, vivacious, play-house style,
That wakes the gay assembly's smile;
Jests that his brother-beaus may hit,
And pass with young Coquettes for wit,
And, priz'd by Fops of true discerning,
Outface the pedantry of learning.   *230*
Yet Learning too shall lend its aid,
To fill the Coxcomb's spongy head,
And studious oft he shall peruse
The labours of the Modern Muse.
From endless loads of Novels gain
Soft, simpring tales of am'rous pain,
With double meanings, neat and handy,
From *Rochester* and *Tristram Shandy.*
The blundering aid of weak Reviews,
That forge the fetters of the muse,   *240*
Shall give him airs of criticizing
On faults of books, he ne'er set eyes on.
The Magazines shall teach the fashion,
And common-place of conversation,
And where his knowledge fails, afford
The aid of many a sounding word.
    Then least Religion he should need,
Of pious *Hume he'll learn his creed,

* *Hume, Voltaire & Bolingbroke* are three of the most noted Deistical
Writers, whose admirers are more numerous, even in *America,* than
perhaps many of our honest Country-readers may imagine. It will
be easily discerned, that my design was to draw a compleat character
of a first-rate Coxcomb, and not to confine myself merely to the inferior, second-handed, imitative Beaus of this country, among whom,
though we can boast of some promising Geniuses, yet Foppery seems
to be but just cleverly dawning.

By strongest demonstration shown,
Evince that nothing can be known; 250
Take arguments, unvex'd by doubt,
On *Voltaire's* trust, or go without;
'Gainst Scripture rail in modern lore,
As thousand fools have rail'd before:
Or pleas'd, a nicer art display
T' expound its doctrines all away,
Suit it to modern taste and fashions
By various notes and emendations;
The rules the ten commands contain,
With new provisos well explain; 260
Prove all Religion was but fashion,
Beneath the Jewish dispensation,
A ceremonious law, deep-hooded
In types and figures long exploded;
Its stubborn fetters all unfit
For these free times of Gospel-light,
This Rake's *Millennium,* since the day
When Sabbaths first were done away;
Since Shame, the worst of deadly fiends,
On Virtue, as its 'Squire, attends; 270
Since Pandar-conscience holds the door,
And lewdness is a vice no more;
And fools may, swift as crimes convey 'em,
Flee to their place, and no man stay 'em.
 Alike his poignant wit displays
The darkness of the former days,
When men the paths of duty sought,
And own'd what revelation taught;
E'er human reason grew so bright,
Men could see all things by its light, 280
And summon'd Scripture to appear,
And stand before its bar severe,
To clear its page from charge of fiction,

And answer pleas of contradiction;
E'er myst'ries first were held in scorn,
Or *Bolingbroke,* or *Hume* were born.
　　And now the Fop, with great energy,
Levels at *Priestcraft* and *the Clergy,*
At *holy cant* and *godly pray'rs,*
And *bigot's hypocritic airs;*　　　　　　　　　　*290*
Musters each vet'ran jest to aid,
Calls Piety *the Parson's trade;*
Cries out 'tis shame, past all abiding,
The world should still be so *Priest-ridden;*
Applauds *free thought,* that scorns controul,
And *gen'rous nobleness of soul,*
That acts its pleasure, good or evil,
And fears nor Deity, nor Devil.
These standing topics never fail
To prompt our little Wits to rail,　　　　　　　　*300*
With mimic droll'ry of grimace,
And pleas'd impertinence of face,
'Gainst Virtue arm their feeble forces,
And sound the charge in peals of curses.
　　Blest be his ashes! (under ground
If any particles be found)
Who, friendly to the Coxcomb-race,
First taught these arts of common-place,
These topics fine, on which the Beau
May all his little wits bestow,　　　　　　　　　　*310*
Secure the simple laugh to raise,
And gain the Dunce's palm of praise.
For where's the theme that Beaus could hit
With least similitude of wit,
Did not Religion and the Priest
Supply materials for the jest?
The poor in purse, with metals vile
For current coins, the world beguile;

The poor in brain, for genuine wit
Pass off a viler counterfeit;   *320*
(While various thus their doom appears,
These lose their souls, and those their ears)
The want of fancy, whim supplies,
And native humour, mad caprice;
Loud noise for argument goes off,
For mirth polite, the ribald's scoff;
For sense, lewd droll'ries entertain us,
And wit is mimick'd by prophaneness.
    Thus 'twixt the Tailor and the Player,
And *Hume,* and *Tristram* and *Voltaire,*   *330*
Complete in modern trim array'd,
The Clockwork-Gentleman is made;
As thousand Fops e'er *Dick* have shone,
In airs, which *Dick* e'er long shall own.
    But not immediate from the Clown,
He gains this zenith of renown;
Slow dawns the Coxcomb's op'ning ray:
Rome was not finish'd in a day.
Perfection is the work of time;
Gradual he mounts the height sublime;   *340*
First shines abroad with bolder grace,
In suits of *second-handed* lace,
And learns by rote, like studious play'rs,
The fop's infinity of airs;
Till merit, to full ripeness grown,
By constancy attains the crown.
    Now should our tale at large proceed,
Here I might tell, and you might read
At college next how *Dick* went on,
And prated much and studied none;   *350*
Yet shone with fair, unborrow'd ray,
And steer'd where nature led the way.
What tho' each academic Science

Bade all his efforts bold defiance!
What tho' in Algebra his station
Was *negative* in each equation;
Tho' in Astronomy survey'd,
His constant course was *retrograde;*
O'er *Newton's* system tho' he sleeps,
And finds his wits in dark eclipse!   *360*
His talents prov'd of highest price
At all the arts of Cards and Dice;
His genius turn'd, with greatest skill,
To whist, loo, cribbage and quadrille,
And taught, to ev'ry rival's shame,
Each nice distinction of the game.
    As noonday sun, the case is plain,
Nature has nothing made in vain.
The blind mole cannot fly; 'tis found
His genius leads him under ground;   *370*
The man, that was not made to think,
Was born to game, and swear, and drink:
Let Fops defiance bid to satire,
Mind *Tully's* rule, and follow nature.
    Yet here the Muse, of *Dick,* must tell
He shone in active scenes as well;
The foremost place in riots held;
In all the gifts of noise excell'd;
His tongue, the bell, whose rattling din wou'd
Summon the Rake's nocturnal synod;   *380*
Swore with a grace, that seem'd design'd
To emulate th' infernal kind,
Nor only make their realms his due,
But learn, betimes, their language too;
And well expert in arts polite,
Drank wine by quarts to mend his sight,
(For he that drinks, till all things reel,
Sees double, and that's twice as well)

And e'er its force confin'd his feet,
Led out his mob to scour the street;   *390*
Made all authority his may game,
And strain'd his little wits to plague 'em.
Then, ev'ry crime aton'd with ease,
Pro meritis receiv'd degrees;
And soon, as fortune chanc'd to fall,
His Father died and left him all:
Then, bent to gain all modern fashions,
He sail'd to visit foreign nations,
Resolv'd, by toil unaw'd, t' import
The follies of the British Court;   *400*
But in his course o'erlook'd whate'er
Was learn'd or valu'd, rich or rare.
   As fire electric draws together
Each hair and straw and dust and feather,
The travell'd Dunce collects betimes
The levities of other climes;
And when long toil has giv'n success,
Returns his native land to bless,
A Patriot-fop, that struts by rules,
And Knight of all the shire of fools.   *410*
   The praise of other learning lost,
To know the world is all his boast,
By conduct teach our Country-wigeons,
How Coxcombs shine in other regions,
Display his travell'd airs and fashions,
And scoff at *College-educations.*
   Whoe'er at College points his sneer,
Proves that *himself* learn'd nothing there,
And wisely makes his honest aim
To pay the mutual debt of shame.   *420*
   Mean while our Hero's anxious care
Was all employ'd to please the Fair;
With vows of love and airs *polite,*

Oft sighing at some Lady's feet;
Pleas'd, while he thus in form addrest her,
With his own gracefulness of gesture,
And gaudy flatt'ry, that displays
A studied elegance of phrase.
So gay at balls the Coxcomb shone,
He thought the Female world his own.   430
By beauty's charms he ne'er was fir'd;
He flatter'd where the world admir'd.
Himself (so well he priz'd desert)
Possest his own unrivall'd heart;
Nor charms, nor chance, nor change could move
The firm foundations of his love:
His heart, so constant and so wise,
Pursued what Sages old advise,
Bade others seek for fame or pelf;
His only study was Himself.   440
    Yet *Dick* allow'd the Fair, desert,
Nor wholly scorn'd them in his heart;
There was an end (as oft he said)
For which alone the Sex were made,
Whereto, of nature's rules observant,
He strove to render them subservient;
And held the Fair by inclination,
Were form'd exactly for their station,
That real virtue ne'er could find
Her lodging in a female mind;   450
Quoted from *Pope,* in phrase so smart,
That all the Sex are "rakes at heart,"
And prais'd *Mahomet's* sense, who holds
That Women ne'er were born with souls.
    Thus blest, our Hero saw his name
Rank'd in the foremost lists of fame.
What tho' the learn'd, the good, the wise,
His light, affected airs despise!

What tho' the Fair, of higher mind,
With brighter thought and sense refin'd,   *460*
Whose fancy rose on nobler wing,
Scorn'd the vain, gilt, gay, noisy thing!
Each light Coquette spread forth her charms,
And lur'd the Hero to her arms.
For Beaus and light Coquettes, by fate
Were each design'd the other's mate,
By instinct love, for each may find
It's likeness in the other's mind;
Then let the wiser sort desert 'em,
For 'twere a sin to try to part 'em.   *470*
    Nor did the coxcomb-loving climate
To these alone his praises limit.
Each gayer Fop of modern days
Allow'd to *Dick* the foremost praise,
Borrow'd his style, his airs, grimace,
And aped his modish form of dress.
Ev'n Some, with sense endued, felt hopes
And rais'd ambition to be fops:
But Men of sense, 'tis fix'd by fate,
Are Coxcombs but of second rate.   *480*
The pert and lively *Dunce* alone
Can steer the course that *Dick* has shown;
The lively Dunce alone can climb
The summit, where he shines sublime.
    But ah! how short the fairest name
Stands on the slipp'ry steep of fame!
The noblest heights we're soonest giddy on:
The sun ne'er stays in his meridian;
The brightest stars must quickly set;
And *Dick* has deeply run in debt.   *490*
Now what avails his splendid show,
With all the arts, that grace the Beau!
Not all his oaths can Duns dismay,

Or deadly Bailiffs fright away;
Not all his compliments can bail,
Or minuets dance him from the jail.
Law not the least respect can give
To the laced coat, or ruffled sleeve.
Off fly at once, in saddest woe,
The dress and trappings of the Beau;   *500*
His splendid ornaments must fall,
And all is lost; for these were all.
    What then remains? in health's decline,
By lewdness, luxury and wine,
Worn by disease, with purse too shallow,
To lead in fashions, or to follow,
The meteor's gaudy light is gone;
Lone Age with hasty step comes on;
The charms he once with pride display'd,
All vanish'd into empty shade;   *510*
And only left, in tawdry show,
The superannuated Beau.
How pale the palsied Fop appears,
Low-shivring in the vale of years;
The ghost of all his former days,
When folly lent the ear of praise.
And Beaus with pleas'd attention hung
On accents of his chatt'ring tongue.
Now all those days of pleasure o'er,
That chatt'ring tongue must prate no more.   *520*
From ev'ry place, that bless'd his hopes,
He's elbow'd out by younger Fops.
Each pleasing thought unknown, that chears
The sadness of declining years,
In lonely age he sinks forlorn,
Of all, and ev'n himself, the scorn.
    The Coxcomb's course were wondrous clever,
Would health and money last forever,

Did Conscience never break the charm,
Nor fears of future worlds alarm.   *530*
    But oh, since youth and years decay,
And life's vain follies fleet away,
Since Age has no respect for Beaus,
And Death the gaudy scene must close,
Happy the Man, whose early bloom
Provides for endless years to come;
That learning seeks, whose useful gain
Repays the course of studious pain,
Whose fame the thankful age shall raise,
And future times repeat its praise;   *540*
Attains that heart-felt peace of mind,
To all the will of heav'n resign'd,
Which calms in youth, the blast of rage,
Adds sweetest hope to sinking age,
With valued use prolongs the breath,
And gives a placid smile to death.
    Then let us scorn the praise that springs
From gaudy, sublunary things.
Hate the vain joys, that vice can claim,
To nobler thoughts exalt our aim,   *550*
With ardour seek th' immortal prize,
And seize our portion in the skies.

PART THIRD, AND LAST

Sometimes called

THE PROGRESS OF COQUETRY

OR

The
Adventures
of
Miss Harriet Simper

OF THE COLONY OF CONNECTICUT

CONTAINING : Advice of the Ladies to Harriet's Mother concerning education—Address to Parents—Harriet's studies, skill in fashions, scandal and romances—with the consequent occurrences of her life by way of illustration of the moral of the work.

*—Quaeq; ipse miserrima vidi,
Et quorum pars magna fui.—*

VIRGIL

For the use of the Ladies and their Parents

AUTHOR'S
PREFACE

Nothing gives more convincing proof of deficiency in judgment or malevolence of heart in an Author, than general, undistinguishing satire, levelled at an order of men, at a sex, or at human nature. Most writers, who have taken the Fair Sex as their subject, have treated them without proper distinction, and either deified them without exceptions, or condemned them without mercy; and scarcely have the Ladies been more exposed by ridiculous flattery, than injured by undeserved censure. The Roman Poet, Juvenal, *who gave the lead to these Lampooners, hath railed at the Sex in a very long satire, the most witty and injudicious of all his productions. The Essay on the Characters of Women by* Pope, *notwithstanding the capricious praises of his whimsical Editor, is one of his least meritorious performances, and was justly received with coldness by the public. Swift, tho' he hath shown far greater knowlege of human nature, hath*

*debased all his satires on the Ladies, by the most general
aspersions and dirty raillery.* Young, *inferior perhaps to the
two last in genius, hath displayed much more judgment and
true wit on these subjects. His satires I would recommend to
the perusal of my fair readers, as the reproofs and corrections
of a friend. The man, who only insults over vice and folly,
without shewing their causes, or pointing out the remedy, em-
ploys his pen to very little purpose: like a physician, who
should prove you had a mortal disease, and yet through malice or ignorance should refuse a prescription.*

*My design in this Poem is to shew, that all the foibles we
discover in the Fair Sex arise principally from the neglect of
their education, and the mistaken notions they imbibe in
their early youth. This naturally introduced a description of
these foibles, which I have endeavoured to laugh at with
good humour, and to expose without malevolence. Had I
only consulted my own taste, I would have preferred sense
and spirit with a style more elevated and poetical, to a per-
petual drollery, and the affectation of wit: but I have found
by experience in the second part of this work, that it is not
so agreeable to the bulk of my readers; and I wished in the
last production I shall probably offer the public to have the
good fortune of general approbation. I have endeavoured to
avoid unseasonable severity, and hope, in that point, I am
pretty clear of censure; especially as some of my good friends
in these parts have lately made a discovery that severity is
not my talent, and there is nothing to be feared from the
strokes of my satire; a discovery, that on this head hath given
me no small consolation. In the following poem, my design
is so apparent, that I am not much afraid of general mis-
representation; and I hope there are no grave folks, who will
think it trifling or unimportant. I expect however, from the
treatment I have already received in regard to the former
parts of this work, as well as some later and more fugitive
productions, that my designs will by many be ignorantly or*

wilfully misunderstood. I shall rest satisfied with the consciousness that a desire to promote the interests of learning and morality was the principal motive, that influenced me in these writings; judging as I did, that unless I attempted something in this way, that might conduce to the service of mankind, I had spent much time in the studies of the Muses in vain.

Polite literature hath within a few years made very considerable advances in America. *Mankind in general seem sensible of the importance and advantages of learning. Female Education hath been most neglected; and I wish this small performance may have some tendency to encourage and promote it. The sprightliness of Female genius, and the excellence of that Sex in their proper walks of science are by no means inferior to the accomplishments of Men. And although the course of their education ought to be different, and writing is not so peculiarly the business of the sex, yet I cannot but hope hereafter to see the accomplishment of my prediction in their favor.*

Her Daughters too this happy land shall grace
With pow'rs of genius, as with charms of face:
Blest with the softness of the female mind,
With fancy blooming, and with taste refin'd,
Some Rowe *shall rise and wrest with daring pen,*
The pride of genius from assuming men;
While each bright line a polish'd beauty wears;
For ev'ry Muse and ev'ry Grace are theirs.

The
Adventures
of
Miss Harriet Simper

"COME HITHER, *Harriet*, pretty Miss,
   Come hither; give your aunt a kiss.
What, blushing? fye, hold up your head.
Full six years old, and yet afraid!
With such a form, an air, a grace,
You're not asham'd to shew your face!
Look like a Lady—bold—my Child—
   Why, Ma'am, your *Harriet* will be spoil'd.
What pity 'tis, a girl so sprightly
Should hang her head so unpolitely?   10
And sure there's nothing worth a rush in
That odd, unnatural trick of blushing;
It marks one ungenteelly bred,
And shows she's mischief in her head.
I've heard *Dick Hairbrain* prove from *Paul*;
Eve never blush'd before the fall.

'Tis said indeed, in later days,
It gain'd our grandmothers some praise;
Perhaps it suited well enough
With hoop and fardingale and ruff;   *20*
But this politer generation
Hold ruffs and blushes out of fashion.
   And what can mean that gown so odd?
You ought to dress her in the mode,
To teach her how to make a figure;
Or she'll be awkward when she's bigger,
And look as queer as *Joan of Nokes*,
And never rig like other folks;
Her cloaths will trail, all fashion lost,
As if she hung them on a post,   *30*
And sit as awkwardly as *Eve's*
First peagreen petticoat of leaves.
   And what can mean your simple whim here
To keep her poring on her primmer?
'Tis quite enough for girls to know,
If she can read a billet-doux,
Or write a line you'd understand
Without an alphabet o' th' hand.
Why needs she learn to write, or spell?
A pothook-scrawl is just as well;   *40*
It ranks her with the better sort,
For 'tis the reigning mode at court.
And why should girls be learn'd or wise?
Books only serve to spoil their eyes.
The studious eye but faintly twinkles,
And reading paves the way to wrinkles.
In vain may learning fill the head full:
'Tis Beauty that's the one thing needful;
Beauty, our sex's sole pretence,
The best receipt for female sense,   *50*
The charm, that turns all words to witty,

And makes the silliest speeches pretty.
Ev'n folly borrows killing graces
From ruby lips and roseate faces.
Give airs and beauty to your daughter,
And sense and wit will follow after."
    Thus round the infant Miss in state
The council of the Ladies meet,
And gay in modern style and fashion
Prescribe their rules of education.   *60*
The Mother, once herself a toast,
Prays for her child the self-same post;
The Father hates the toil and pother,
And leaves his daughters to their mother;
A proper hand their youth to guide,
And o'er their studies to preside;
From whom her faults, that never vary,
May come by right hereditary,
Follies be multiplied with quickness,
And whims keep up the family likeness.   *70*
    Ye Parents, shall those forms so fair,
The Graces might be proud to wear,
The charms those speaking eyes display,
Where passion sits in ev'ry ray,
Th' expressive glance, the air refin'd,
That sweet vivacity of mind,
Be doom'd for life to folly's sway,
By trifles lur'd, to fops a prey,
Blank all the pow'rs that nature gave,
To dress and tinsel-show the slave!   *80*
Say, can ye think that charms so bright,
Were giv'n alone to please the sight,
Or like the moon, that forms so fine
Were made for nothing but to shine?
With lips of rose and cheeks of cherry,
Out go the works of statuary?

And gain the prize of show, as victors
O'er busts and effigies and pictures?
Can female Sense no trophies raise?
Are dress and beauty all their praise?   *90*
And does no lover hope to find
An angel in his charmer's mind?
First from the dust our sex began:
But woman was refin'd from man;
Receiv'd again, with softer air,
The great Creator's forming care.
And shall it no attention claim
Their beauteous infant souls to frame?
Shall half your precepts tend the while
Fair nature's lovely work to spoil,   *100*
The native innocence deface,
The glowing blush, the modest grace,
On follies fix their young desire,
To trifles bid their souls aspire,
Fill their gay heads with whims of fashion,
And slight all other cultivation,
Let ev'ry useless barren weed
Of foolish fancy run to seed,
And make their minds the receptacle
Of ev'ry thing that's false and fickle,   *110*
Where gay Caprice with wanton air,
And Vanity keep constant fair,
Where ribbands, laces, patches, puffs,
Caps, jewels, ruffles, tippets, muffs,
With gaudy whims of vain parade,
Croud each apartment of the head,
Where stands display'd with costly pains
The toyshop of Coquettish brains,
And high-crown'd caps hang out the sign,
And beaus, as customers throng in;   *120*
Whence Sense is banish'd in disgrace,

Where Wisdom dares not shew her face,
Where calm Reflection cannot live,
Nor thought sublime an hour survive;
Where the light head and vacant brain
Spoil all ideas they contain,
As th' airpump kills in half a minute
Each living thing you put within it.
    It must be so; by antient rule
The Fair are nurst in Folly's school,   *130*
And all their education done
Is none at all, or worse than none;
Whence still proceed in maid or wife,
The follies and the ills of life.
Learning is call'd our mental diet,
That serves the hungry mind to quiet,
That gives the genius fresh supplies,
Till souls grow up to common size:
But here, despising sense refin'd,
Gay trifles feed the youthful mind.   *140*
Chamaeleons thus, whose colours airy
As often as Coquettes can vary,
Despise all dishes rich and rare,
And diet wholly on the air;
Think fogs blest eating, nothing finer,
And can on whirlwinds make a dinner;
And thronging all to feast together,
Fare daintily in blustring weather.
    Here to the Fair alone remain
Long years of action spent in vain;   *150*
In numbers little skill it shows
To cast the sum of all she knows.
Perhaps she learns (what can she less?)
The arts of dancing and of dress.
But dress and dancing are to women,
Their education's mint and cummin;

These lighter graces should be taught,
And weightier matters not forgot.
For there, where only these are shown,
The soul will fix on these alone.   *160*
Then most the fineries of dress
Her thoughts, her wish and time possess;
She values only to be gay,
And works to rig herself for play;
Weaves scores of caps with diff'rent spires,
And all varieties of wires;
Gay ruffles varying just as flow'd
The tides and ebbings of the mode;
Bright flow'rs, and topknots waving high,
That float, like streamers in the sky;   *170*
Work'd catgut handkerchiefs, whose flaws
Display the neck, as well as gauze;
Or network aprons somewhat thinnish,
That cost but six weeks time to finish,
And yet so neat, as you must own
You could not buy for half a crown—
Perhaps in youth (for country-fashions
Prescrib'd that mode of educations)
She wastes long months in still more tawdry,
And useless labours of embroid'ry;   *180*
With toil weaves up for chairs together,
Six bottoms quite as good as leather;
A set of curtains tap'stry work,
The figures frowning like the Turk;
A tentstitch picture, work of folly,
With portraits wrought of *Dick* and *Polly*;
A coat of arms, that mark'd her house,
Three owls rampant, the crest a goose:
Or shews in waxwork Goodman *Adam*,
And Serpent gay, gallanting Madam,   *190*
A woeful mimickry of *Eden*,

With fruit, that needs not be forbidden:
All useless works, that fill for Beauties
Of time and sense their vast vacuities;
Of sense, which reading might bestow,
And time, whose worth they never know.
    Now to some pop'lous city sent,
She comes back prouder than she went;
Few months in vain parade she spares,
Nor learns, but apes, politer airs;   200
So formal acts, with such a set air,
That country-manners far were better.
This springs from want of just discerning,
As pedantry from want of learning;
And proves this maxim true to sight,
The half-genteel are least polite.
    Yet still that active spark, the mind
Employment constantly will find,
And when on trifles most 'tis bent,
Is always found most diligent;   210
For, weighty works men shew most sloth in,
But labour hard at *Doing Nothing*,
A trade, that needs no deep concern,
Or long apprenticeship to learn,
To which mankind at first apply
As naturally as to cry,
Till at the last their latest groan
Proclaims their idleness is done.
Good sense, like fruits, is rais'd by toil;
But follies sprout in ev'ry soil,   220
And where no tillage finds a place,
They grow, like tares, the more apace,
Nor culture, pains, nor planting need,
As moss and mushrooms have no seed.
    Thus *Harriet*, rising on the stage,
Learns all the arts, that please the age,

And studies well, as fits her station,
The trade and politics of fashion:
A judge of modes, in silks and sattens,
From tassels down to clogs and pattens;   230
A genius, that can calculate
When modes of dress are out of date,
Cast the nativity with ease
Of gowns, and sacks and negligees,
And tell, exact to half a minute,
What's out of fashion and what's in it;
And scanning all with curious eye
Minutest faults in dresses spy;
(So in nice points of sight, a flea
Sees atoms better far than we,)   240
A Patriot too, she greatly labours,
To spread her arts amongs her neighbours,
Holds correspondencies to learn
What facts the female world concern,
To gain authentic state-reports
Of varied modes in distant courts,
The present state and swift decays
Of tuckers, handkerchiefs and stays,
The colour'd silk that Beauties wraps,
And all the rise and fall of caps.   250
Then shines, a pattern to the fair,
Of mein, address and modish air,
Of ev'ry new, affected grace,
That plays the eye, or decks the face,
The artful smile, that beauty warms,
And all th' hypocrisy of charms.
    On sunday see the haughty Maid
In all the glare of dress aray'd,
Deck'd in her most fantastic gown,
Because a stranger's come to town.   260
Heedless at church she spends the day

For homelier folks may serve to pray,
And for devotion those may go,
Who can have nothing else to do.
Beauties at church must spend their care in
Far other work, than pious hearing;
They've Beaus to conquer, Belles to rival;
To make them serious were uncivil.
For, like the preacher, they each sunday
Must do their whole week's work in one day.   *270*

   As tho' they meant to take by blows
Th' opposing galleries of Beaus,
To church the female Squadron move,
All arm'd with weapons used in love.
Like colour'd ensigns gay and fair,
High caps rise floating in the air;
Bright silk its varied radiance flings,
And streamers wave in kissing-strings;
Their darts and arrows are not seen,
But lovers tell us what they mean;   *280*
Each bears th' artill'ry of her charms,
Like training bands at viewing arms.

   So once, in fear of Indian beating,
Our grandsires bore their guns to meeting,
Each man equipp'd on sunday morn,
With psalm-book, shot and powder-horn;
And look'd in form, as all must grant,
Like th' antient, true church militant;
Or fierce, like modern deep Divines,
Who fight with quills, like porcupines.   *290*

   Or let us turn the style and see
Our Belles assembled o'er their tea;
Where folly sweetens ev'ry theme,
And scandal serves for sugar'd cream.

   "And did you hear the news? (they cry)
The court wear caps full three feet high,

Built gay with wire, and at the end on't,
Red tassels streaming like a pendant:
Well sure, it must be vastly pretty;
'Tis all the fashion in the city.   *300*
And were you at the ball last night?
Well *Chloe* look'd like any fright;
Her day is over for a toast;
She'd now do best to act a ghost.
You saw our *Fanny*; envy must own
She figures, since she came from *Boston*,
Good company improves one's air—
I think the troops were station'd there.
Poor *Caelia* ventur'd to the place;
The small-pox quite has spoil'd her face.   *310*
A sad affair, we all confest:
But providence knows what is best.
Poor *Dolly* too, that writ the letter
Of love to *Dick*; but *Dick* knew better;
A secret that; you'll not disclose it:
There's not a person living knows it.
Sylvia shone out, no peacock finer;
I wonder what the fops see in her.
Perhaps 'tis true, what *Harry* maintains,
She mends on *intimate acquaintance*."   *320*
    Hail British Lands! to whom belongs
Untroubled privilege of tongues,
Blest gift of freedom, priz'd as rare
By all, but dearest to the fair;
From grandmothers of loud renown,
Thro' long succession handed down,
Thence with affection kind and hearty,
Bequeath'd unlessen'd to poster'ty!
And all ye Pow'rs of slander, hail,
Who teach to censure and to rail!   *330*
By you, kind aids to prying eyes,

Minutest faults the fair one spies,
And specks in rival toasts can mind,
Which no one else could ever find;
By shrewdest hints and doubtful guesses,
Tears reputations all in pieces;
Points out what smiles to sin advance,
Find assignations in a glance;
And shews how rival toasts (you'll think)
Break all commandments with a wink.   340
 So Priests drive poets to the lurch
By fulminations of the church,
Mark in our titlepage our crimes,
Find heresies in double rhymes,
Charge tropes with damnable opinion,
And prove a metaphor *Arminian*,
Peep for our doctrines, as at windows,
And pick out creeds of inneundoes.
 And now the conversation sporting
From scandal turns to trying fortune.   350
Their future luck the fair foresee
In dreams, in cards, but most in tea.
Each finds of love some future trophy
In settlings left of tea, or coffee:
There fate displays its book, she believes,
And Lovers swim in form of tea-leaves;
Where oblong stalks she takes for Beaus,
And squares of leaves for billet-doux,
Gay balls in parboil'd fragments rise,
And specks for kisses greet her eyes.   360
 So Roman Augurs wont to pry
In victims hearts for prophecy,
Sought from the future world advices,
By lights and lungs of sacrifices,
And read with eyes more sharp than wizards,
The book of fate in pigeon's gizzards;

Could tell what chief would be survivor,
From aspects of an oxes liver,
And cast what luck would fall in fights,
By trine and quartile of its lights.   *370*
    Yet that we fairly may proceed,
We own that Ladies sometimes read,
And grieve *that* reading is confin'd
To books that poison all the mind;
The bluster of romance, that fills
The head brimfull of purling rills,
Inspires with dreams the witless maiden
On flow'ry vales, and fields Arcadian,
And swells the mind with haughty fancies,
And am'rous follies of romances,   *380*
With whims that in no place exist,
But author's heads and woman's breast.
    For while she reads romance, the Fair one
Fails not to think herself the Heroine;
For ev'ry glance, or smile, or grace,
She finds resemblance in her face,
Thinks while the fancied beauties strike,
Two peas were never more alike,
Expects the world to fall before her,
And ev'ry fop she meets adore her.   *390*
    Thus *Harriet* reads, and reading really
Believes herself a young *Pamela*,
The high-wrought whim, the tender strain
Elate her mind and turn her brain:
Before her glass, with smiling grace,
She views the wonders of her face;
There stands in admiration moveless,
And hopes a *Grandison*, or *Lovelace*.
    Then shines She forth, and round her hovers
The powder'd swarm of bowing Lovers;   *400*
By flames of love attracted thither,

Fops, scholars, dunces, cits, together.
No lamp expos'd in nightly skies
E'er gather'd such a swarm of flies;
Or flame in tube electric draws
Such thronging multitudes of straws.
(For I shall still take similes
From *fire electric* when I please.)
    With vast confusion swells the sound,
When all the Coxcombs flutter round.   *410*
What undulation wide of bows!
What gentle oaths and am'rous vows!
What doubl' entendres all so smart!
What sighs hot-piping from the heart!
What jealous leers! what angry brawls
To gain the Lady's hand at balls!
What billet-doux, brimful of flame!
Acrostics lined with *Harriet's* name!
What compliments o'erstrain'd with telling
Sad lies of *Venus* and of *Hellen*!   *420*
What wits half-crack'd with common places
On angels, goddesses and graces!
On fires of love what witty puns!
What similes of stars and suns!
What cringing, dancing, ogling, sighing,
What languishing for love, and dying!
    For Lovers of all things that breathe
Are most expos'd to sudden death,
And many a swain much fam'd in rhymes
Hath died some hundred thousand times: *430*
Yet tho' love oft their breath may stifle,
'Tis sung it hurts them but a trifle.
The swain revives by equal wonder,
As snakes will join when cut asunder,
And often murther'd still survives;
No cat hath half so many lives.

While round the fair, the Coxcombs throng
With oath, card, billet-doux, and song,
She spread her charms and wish'd to gain
The heart of ev'ry simple swain;   *440*
To all with gay, alluring air,
She hid in smiles the fatal snare,
For sure that snare must fatal prove,
Where falshood wears the form of love;
Full oft with pleasing transport hung
On accents of each flattring tongue,
And found a pleasure most sincere
From each erect, attentive ear;
For pride was hers, that oft with ease,
Despis'd the man, she wish'd to please.   *450*
She lov'd the chace, but scorn'd the prey,
And fish'd for hearts to throw away;
Joy'd at the tale of piercing darts,
And tortring flames and pining hearts,
And pleas'd perus'd the billet-doux,
That said, "I die for love of you;"
Found conquest in each gallant's sighs,
And blest the murders of her eyes.
    So Doctors live but by the dead,
And pray for plagues, as daily bread;   *460*
Thank providence for colds and fevers,
And hold consumptions special favors;
And think diseases kindly made,
As blest materials of their trade.
    'Twould weary all the pow'rs of verse
Their am'rous speeches to rehearse,
Their compliments, whose vain parade
Turns *Venus* to a kitchen-maid;
With high pretence of love and honor,
They vent their folly all upon her,   *470*
(Ev'n as the scripture-precept saith,

More shall be given to him that hath;)
Tell her how *wondrous* fair they deem her,
How handsome all the world esteem her;
And while they flatter and adore,
She contradicts to call for more.
   "And did they say I was so handsome?
My looks—I'm sure no one can fancy 'em.
'Tis true we're all as we were fram'd,
And none have right to be asham'd;   *480*
But as for beauty—all can tell
I never fancied I look'd well;
I were a fright, had I a grain less.
You're only joking, Mr. *Brainless*."
   Yet Beauty still maintain'd her sway;
And bade the proudest hearts obey;
Ev'n Sense her glances could beguile,
And vanquish'd Wisdom with a smile:
While Merit bow'd and found no arms,
T'oppose the conquest of her charms,   *490*
Caught all those bashful fears, that place
The mask of folly on the face,
That awe, that robs our airs of ease,
And blunders, when it hopes to please;
For men of sense will always prove
The most forlorn of fools in love.
The fair esteem'd, admir'd, 'tis true,
And prais'd—'tis all Coquettes can do.
   And when deserving Lovers came
Believ'd her smiles and own'd their flame,   *500*
Her bosom thrill'd, with joy affected
T' increase the list, she had rejected;
While pleas'd to see her arts prevail,
To each she told the self-same tale.
She wish'd in truth they ne'er had seen her,
And feign'd what grief it oft had giv'n her,

And sad, of tender-hearted make,
Griev'd they were ruin'd for her sake.
'Twas true, she own'd on recollection,
She'd giv'n them proofs of kind affection: *510*
But they mistook her whole intent,
For friendship was the thing she meant.
She wonder'd how their hearts could move 'em
So strangely as to think she'd love 'em;
She thought her purity above
The low and sensual flames of love;
And yet they made such sad ado,
She wish'd she could have lov'd them too.
She pitied them and as a friend
She priz'd them more than all mankind;   *520*
And begg'd them not their hearts to vex,
Or hang themselves, or break their necks;
Told them 'twould make her life uneasy,
If they should run forlorn, or crazy:
Objects of *love* she could not deem 'em;
But did most marv'lously *esteem* 'em.
    For 'tis *Esteem*, Coquettes dispense
Tow'rd learning, genius, worth and sense,
Sincere affection, truth refin'd,
And all the merit of the mind.   *530*
    But *Love's* the passion they experience
For gold, and dress, and gay appearance.
    For ah! what magic charms and graces
Are found in golden suits of laces!
What going forth of hearts and souls
Tow'rd glares of gilded button-holes!
What Lady's heart can stand its ground
'Gainst hats with glittring edging bound?
While vests and shoes and hose conspire,
And gloves and ruffles fan the fire;   *540*
And broadcloths, cut by tailor's arts,

Spread fatal nets for female hearts.
   And oh, what charms more potent shine,
Drawn from the dark Peruvian mine!
What spells and talismans of *Venus*
Are found in dollars, crowns and guineas!
In purse of gold, a single stiver
Beats all the darts in *Cupid*'s quiver.
What heart so constant, but must veer,
When drawn by thousand pounds a year!   550
How many fair ones ev'ry day
To houses fine have fall'n a prey;
Been forced on stores of goods to fix,
Or carried off in coach and six!
For *Caelia* merit found no dart;
Five thousand sterling broke her heart.
So witches, hunters say confound 'em,
For silver bullets only wound 'em.
   Cupid of old, as poets say,
But barter'd hearts in simple way;   560
Our modern *Cupid*'s wiser found,
And goes to work on surer ground,
Like Lawyers joins the monied faction,
Thinks gold the surest cause of action,
But where of money not a copper is,
Rejects all suits *in forma pauperis*;
Admits the rich to bliss and glory,
And sends the poor to purgatory.
   And now the time was come, our Fair
Should all the plagues of passion share,   570
And after ev'ry heart she'd won,
By sad disaster lose her own.
So true the antient proverb sayeth,
"Edge tools are dang'rous things to play with;"
The fisher, ev'ry gudgeon hooking,
May chance himself to catch a ducking;

The child that plays with fire, in pain
Will burn its fingers now and then;
And from the Dutchess to the laundress,
Coquets are seldom salamanders.   580
　　For lo! *Dick Hairbrain* heaves in sight,
From foreign climes returning bright,
A Coxcomb, past all mortal matching,
Well worth a Lady's pains in catching;
He danc'd, he sung to admiration;
He swore to gen'ral acceptation;
In airs and dress so great his merit,
He shone—no Lady's eyes could bear it.
Poor *Harriet* saw; her heart was stouter;
She gather'd all her smiles about her;   590
Hoped by her eyes to gain the laurels,
And charm him down, as snakes do squirrels;
So priz'd his love and wish'd to win it,
That all her hopes were center'd in it;
And took such pains his heart to move,
Herself fell desp'rately in love;
Nor had the art to keep it private,
Dick soon found what she meant to drive at.
Tho' great her skill in am'rous tricks,
She could not hope to equal *Dick*'s: 600
Her fate she ventur'd on his trial,
And lost her birthright of denial.
　　And here her brightest hopes miscarry;
For *Dick* was too gallant to marry:
He own'd she'd charms for those who need 'em,
But he, be sure, was all for freedom;
So, left in hopeless flames to burn,
Gay *Dick esteem'd* her in her turn.
　　In love, a Lady once giv'n over
Is never fated to recover,   610
Doom'd to indulge her troubled fancies

And feed her passion by romances;
And always am'rous, always changing,
From coxcomb still to coxcomb ranging,
Finds in her heart a void, which still
Succeeding Beaus can never fill:
As shadows vary o'er a glass,
Each holds in turn the vacant place;
She doats upon her earliest pain,
And following thousands loves in vain.   620

    Poor *Harriet* now hath had her day;
No more the Beaus confess her sway;
New Beauties push her from the stage;
She trembles at th' approach of age,
And starts to view the alter'd face,
That wrinkles at her in her glass:
So *Satan*, in the monk's tradition,
Fear'd, when he met his apparition.

    At length her name each Coxcomb cancels
From standing lists of toasts and angels;   630
And slighted where she shone before,
A grace and goddess now no more,
Depriv'd of long-accustom'd pleasure
In daily falshoods told to praise her;
Despis'd by all, and doom'd to meet
Her lovers at her rival's feet,
She flies assemblies, shuns the ball,
And cries out, Vanity, on all;
Affects to scorn the tinsel-shows
Of glittring Belles and gaudy Beaus;   640
Nor longer hopes to hide by dress
The tracks of age upon her face.
Now careless grown of airs polite,
Her noonday nightcap meets the sight;
Her hair uncomb'd collects together,
With ornament of many a feather;

Her stays for easiness thrown by,
Her rumpled handkerchief awry,
A careless figure half undrest,
(The reader's wits may guess the rest)   *650*
All points of dress and neatness carried,
As tho' she'd been a twelvemonth married;
She spends her breath, as years prevail,
At this sad, wicked world to rail,
To slander all her sex *impromptu*,
And wonder what the times will come to.
   Tom Brainless at the close of last year
Had been six years a rev'rend Pastor,
And now resolv'd to smooth his life,
To seek the blessing of a wife.   *660*
His brethren saw his am'rous temper,
And recommended fair *Miss Simper*,
Who fond, they heard, of sacred truth,
Had left her levities of youth,
Grown fit for th' ministerial union,
And grave, as *Christian*'s wife in *Bunyan*.
   On this he rigg'd him in his best,
And got his old grey wig new-drest,
Fix'd on his suit of sable stuffs,
And brush'd the powder from the cuffs,   *670*
With black silk stockings, yet in being,
The same he took his first degree in;
Procur'd a horse of breed from *Europe*,
And learn'd to mount him by the stirrup,
And set forth fierce to court the Maid;
His white hair'd Deacon went for aid;
And on the right in solemn mode,
The Reverend *Mr. Brainless* rode.
Thus grave, the courtly pair advance,
Like knight and squire in fam'd romance;   *680*
The Priest then bow'd in sober gesture,

And all in scripture terms addrest her;
He'd found for reasons amply known,
It was not good to be alone,
And thought his duty led to trying
The great command of multiplying;
So with submission, by her leave,
He'd come to look him out an *Eve*,
And hoped, in pilgrimage of life,
To find an helpmeet in a wife,   *690*
A wife discreet and fair withal,
To make amends for *Adam*'s fall.
     In short, the bargain finish'd soon,
A reverend Doctor made them one.
     And now the joyful people rouze all
To celebrate their Priest's espousal;
And first, by kind agreement set,
In case their Priest a wife could get,
The parish vote him five pounds clear,
T' increase his salary every year.   *700*
Then swift the tagrag gentry come
To welcome *Madam Brainless* home;
Wish their good Parson joy; with pride
In order round salute the bride;
At home, at visits and at meetings,
To *Madam* all allow precedence:
Greet her at church with rev'rence due,
And next the pulpit fix her pew.—

M'FINGAL

A MODERN EPIC POEM

M'FINGAL

A MODERN EPIC POEM
IN FOUR CANTOS

Ergo non satis est risu diducere rictum
Auditoris: et est quaedam tamen hic quoque virtus.
Est brevitate opus, ut currat sententia, neu se
Impediat verbis lassas onerantibus aures.
Et sermone opus est modo tristi, saepe jocoso,
Defendente vicem modo Rhetoris, atque Poetae,
Interdum urbani parcentis viribus atque
Extenuantis eas consulto. Ridiculum acri
Fortius et melius magnas plerumque secat res.

HORAT. LIB. I. SAT. 10.

With illustrations taken from the edition of 1795,
designed and engraved by E. TISDALE

The
Town Meeting
A.M.

WHEN YANKIES, skill'd in martial rule,
　　First put the British troops to school;
Instructed them in warlike trade,
And new manoeuvres of parade;
The true war-dance of Yanky-reels,
And *manual exercise* of heels;
Made them give up, like saints complete,
The arm of flesh and trust the feet,
And work, like Christians undissembling,
Salvation out, by fear and trembling;　　　　　*10*
Taught Percy fashionable races,
And modern modes of Chevy-chaces:
From Boston, in his best array,
Great 'Squire M'Fingal took his way,
And graced with ensigns of renown,
Steer'd homeward to his native town.

His high descent our heralds trace
To *Ossian's famed Fingalian race:
For tho' their name some part may lack,
Old Fingal spelt it with a Mac;   *20*
Which great M'Pherson, with submission
We hope will add, the next edition.
   His fathers flourish'd in the Highlands
Of Scotia's fog-benighted islands;
Whence gain'd our 'Squire two gifts by right,
Rebellion and the Second-sight.
Of these the first, in ancient days,
Had gain'd the noblest palms of praise,
'Gainst Kings stood forth and many a crown'd head
With terror of its might confounded;   *30*
Till rose a King with potent charm
His foes by goodness to disarm,
Whom ev'ry Scot and Jacobite
Straight fell in love with, at first sight;
Whose gracious speech, with aid of pensions,
Hush'd down all murmurs of dissensions,
And with the sound of potent metal,
Brought all their blust'ring swarms to settle;
Who rain'd his ministerial mannas,
Till loud Sedition sung hosannahs;   *40*
The good Lords-Bishops and the Kirk
United in the public work;
Rebellion from the Northern regions,
With Bute and Mansfield swore allegiance;
And all combin'd to raze as nuisance,
Of church and state, the constitutions;
Pull down the empire, on whose ruins
They meant to edify their new ones;

* See Fingal, an antient Epic Poem, published as the work of Ossian,
a Caledonian Bard, of the third century, by James M'Pherson, a
Scotch ministerial scribbler.

Enslave th' Amer'can wildernesses,
And tear the provinces in pieces.   *50*
For these our 'Squire among the valiant'st,
Employ'd his time and tools and talents;
And in their cause with manly zeal
Used his first virtue, to rebel;
And found this new rebellion pleasing
As his old king-destroying treason.
    Nor less avail'd his optic sleight,
And Scottish gift of second-sight.
No antient sybil fam'd in rhyme
Saw deeper in the womb of time;   *60*
No block in old Dodona's grove,
Could ever more orac'lar prove.
Nor only saw he all that was,
But much that never came to pass;
Whereby all Prophets far outwent he,
Tho' former days produc'd a plenty:
For any man with half an eye,
What stands before him may espy;
But optics sharp it needs I ween,
To see what is not to be seen.   *70*
As in the days of antient fame
Prophets and poets were the same,
And all the praise that poets gain
Is but for what th' invent and feign:
So gain'd our 'Squire his fame by seeing
Such things as never would have being.
Whence he for oracles was grown
The very †tripod of his town.
Gazettes no sooner rose a lye in,
But straight he fell to prophesying;   *80*
Made dreadful slaughter in his course,

† The Tripod was a sacred three-legged stool, from which the antient priests uttered their oracles.

O'erthrew provincials, foot and horse;
Brought armies o'er by sudden pressings
Of Hanoverians, Swiss and Hessians;
Feasted with blood his Scottish clan,
And hang'd all rebels, to a man;
Divided their estates and pelf,
And took a goodly share himself.
All this with spirit energetic,
He did by second-sight prophetic.   *90*
    Thus stor'd with intellectual riches,
Skill'd was our 'Squire in making speeches,
Where strength of brains united centers
With strength of lungs surpassing Stentor's.
But as some musquets so contrive it,
As oft to miss the mark they drive at,
And tho' well aim'd at duck or plover,
Bear wide and kick their owners over:
So far'd our 'Squire, whose reas'ning toil
Would often on himself recoil,   *100*
And so much injur'd more his side,
The stronger arg'ments he applied:
As old war-elephants dismay'd,
Trode down the troops they came to aid,
And hurt their own side more in battle
Than less and ordinary cattle.
Yet at town-meetings ev'ry chief
Pinn'd faith on great M'Fingal's sleeve,
And as he motion'd, all by rote
Rais'd sympathetic hands to vote.   *110*
    The town, our Hero's scene of action,
Had long been torn by feuds of faction,
And as each party's strength prevails,
It turn'd up diff'rent, heads or tails;
With constant rattl'ing in a trice
Show'd various sides as oft as dice:

As that fam'd weaver, *wife t' Ulysses,
By night each day's-work pick'd in pieces,
And tho' she stoutly did bestir her,
Its finishing was ne'er the nearer: *120*
So did this town with stedfast zeal
Weave cob-webs for the public weal,
Which when compleated, or before,
A second vote in pieces tore.
They met, made speeches full long winded,
Resolved, protested, and rescinded;
Addresses sign'd, then chose Committees,
To stop all drinking of Bohea-teas;
With winds of doctrine veer'd about,
And turn'd all Whig-Committees out.   *130*
Meanwhile our Hero, as their head,
In pomp the tory faction led,
Still following, as the 'Squire should please,
Successive on, like files of geese.
    And now the town was summon'd greeting,
To grand parading of town-meeting;
A show, that strangers might appall,
As Rome's grave senate did the Gaul.
High o'er the rout, on pulpit-stairs,
Like den of thieves in house of pray'rs,   *140*
(That house, which loth a rule to break,
Serv'd heav'n but one day in the week,
Open the rest for all supplies
Of news and politics and lies)
Stood forth the constable, and bore
His staff, like Merc'ry's wand of yore,
Wav'd potent round, the peace to keep,
As that laid dead men's souls to sleep.
Above and near th' hermetic staff,

* Homer's Odyssey.

The moderator's upper half,   *150*
In grandeur o'er the cushion bow'd,
Like Sol half-seen behind a cloud.
Beneath stood voters of all colours,
Whigs, tories, orators and bawlers,
With ev'ry tongue in either faction,
Prepar'd, like minute-men, for action;
Where truth and falsehood, wrong and right,
Draw all their legions out to fight;
With equal uproar, scarcely rave
Opposing winds in Aeolus' cave;   *160*
Such dialogues with earnest face,
Held never Balaam with his ass.
    With daring zeal and courage blest
Honorius first the crowd address'd;
When now our 'Squire returning late,
Arrived to aid the grand debate,
With strange sour faces sat him down,
While thus the orator went on.
    "—For ages blest, thus Britain rose
The terror of encircling foes;   *170*
Her heroes rul'd the bloody plain;
Her conq'ring standard aw'd the main:
The diff'rent palms her triumphs grace,
Of arms in war, of arts in peace:
Unharrass'd by maternal care,
Each rising province flourish'd fair;
Whose various wealth with lib'ral hand,
By far o'er-paid the parent-land.
But tho' so bright her sun might shine,
'Twas quickly hasting to decline,   *180*
With feeble rays, too weak t' assuage,
The damps, that chill the eve of age.
    For states, like men, are doom'd as well
Th' infirmities of age to feel;

And from their diff'rent forms of empire
Are seiz'd with ev'ry deep distemper.
Some states high fevers have made head in,
Which nought could cure but copious bleeding;
While others have grown dull and dozy,
Or fix'd in helpless idiocy;   *190*
Or turn'd demoniacs to belabour
Each peaceful habitant and neighbour;
Or vex'd with hypocondriac fits,
Have broke their strength and lost their wits.
   Thus now while hoary years prevail,
Good Mother Britain seem'd to fail;
Her back bent, crippled with the weight
Of age and debts and cares of state:
For debts she ow'd, and those so large,
As twice her wealth could not discharge,   *200*
And now 'twas thought, so high they'd grown,
She'd break and come upon the town;
Her arms, of nations once the dread,
She scarce could lift above her head;
Her deafen'd ears ('twas all their hope)
The final trump perhaps might ope,
So long they'd been in stupid mood,
Shut to the hearing of all good;
Grim Death had put her in his scroll,
Down on the execution-roll;   *210*
And Gallic crows, as she grew weaker,
Began to whet their beaks to pick her.
And now her pow'rs decaying fast,
Her grand Climact'ric had she past,
And, just like all old women else,
Fell in the vapours much by spells.
Strange whimsies on her fancy struck,
And gave her brain a dismal shock;
Her mem'ry fails, her judgment ends;

She quite forgot her nearest friends,   *220*
Lost all her former sense and knowledge,
And fitted fast for Beth'lem college;
Of all the pow'rs she once retain'd,
Conceit and pride alone remain'd.
As Eve when falling was so modest
To fancy she should grow a goddess;
As madmen, straw who long have slept on,
Will stile them, Jupiter or Neptune:
So Britain 'midst her airs so flighty,
Now took a whim to be Almighty;   *230*
Urg'd on to desp'rate heights of frenzy,
Affirm'd her own Omnipotency;
Would rather ruin all her race,
Than 'bate Supremacy an ace;
Assumed all rights divine, as grown
The churches head, like good Pope Joan;
Swore all the world should bow and skip
To her almighty Goodyship;
Anath'matiz'd each unbeliever,
And vow'd to live and rule forever.   *240*
Her servants humour'd every whim,
And own'd at once her pow'r supreme,
Her follies pleas'd in all their stages,
For fake of legacies and wages;
In *Stephen's Chapel* then in state too
Set up her golden calf to pray to,
Proclaim'd its pow'r and right divine,
And call'd for worship at its shrine,
And for poor Heretics to burn us
Bade North prepare his fiery furnace;   *250*
Struck bargains with the Romish churches
Infallibility to purchase;

* The Parliament House is called by that name.

Set wide for Popery the door,
Made friends with Babel's scarlet whore,
Join'd both the matrons firm in clan;
No sisters made a better span.
No wonder then, ere this was over,
That she should make her children suffer.
She first, without pretence of reason,
Claim'd right whate'er we had to seize on;   *260*
And with determin'd resolution,
To put her claims in execution,
Sent fire and sword, and called it, Lenity,
Starv'd us, and christen'd it, Humanity.
For she, her case grown desperater,
Mistook the plainest things in nature;
Had lost all use of eyes or wits;
Took slav'ry for the bill of rights;
Trembled at Whigs and deem'd them foes,
And stopp'd at loyalty her nose;   *270*
Stiled her own children, brats and caitiffs,
And knew us not from th' Indian natives.
    What tho' with supplicating pray'r
We begg'd our lives and goods she'd spare;
Not vainer vows, with sillier call,
Elijah's prophets rais'd to Baal;
A worshipp'd stock of god, or goddess,
Had better heard and understood us.
So once Egyptians at the Nile
Ador'd their guardian Crocodile,   *280*
Who heard them first with kindest ear,
And ate them to reward their pray'r;
And could he talk, as kings can do,
Had made as gracious speeches too.
    Thus spite of pray'rs her schemes pursuing,
She still went on to work our ruin;
Annull'd our charters of releases,

And tore our title-deeds in pieces;
Then sign'd her warrants of ejection,
And gallows rais'd to stretch our necks on: *290*
And on these errands sent in rage,
Her bailiff, and her hangman, Gage,
And at his heels, like dogs to bait us,
Dispatch'd her *Posse Comitatus.*
   No state e'er chose a fitter person,
To carry such a silly farce on.
As Heathen gods in antient days
Receiv'd at second-hand their praise,
Stood imag'd forth in stones and stocks,
And deified in barber's blocks;   *300*
So Gage was chose to represent
Th' omnipotence of Parliament.
And as old heroes gain'd, by shifts,
From gods, as poets tell, their gifts;
Our Gen'ral, as his actions show,
Gain'd like assistance from below,
By Satan graced with full supplies,
From all his magazine of lies.
Yet could his practice ne'er impart
The wit to tell a lie with art.   *310*
Those lies alone are formidable,
Where artful truth is mixt with fable;
But Gage has bungled oft so vilely
No soul would credit lies so silly,
Outwent all faith and stretch'd beyond
Credulity's extremest end.
Whence plain it seems tho' Satan once
O'erlook'd with scorn each brainless dunce,
And blund'ring brutes in Eden shunning,
Chose out the serpent for his cunning;   *320*
Of late he is not half so nice,
Nor picks assistants, 'cause they're wise.

For had he stood upon perfection,
His present friends had lost th' election,
And far'd as hard in this proceeding,
As owls and asses did in Eden.
    Yet fools are often dang'rous enemies,
As meanest reptiles are most venomous;
Nor e'er could Gage by craft and prowess
Have done a whit more mischief to us: *330*
Since he began th' unnatural war,
The work his masters sent him for.
    And are there in this freeborn land
Among ourselves a venal band,
A dastard race, who long have sold
Their souls and consciences for gold;
Who wish to stab their country's vitals,
If they might heir surviving titles;
With joy behold our mischiefs brewing,
Insult and triumph in our ruin?   *340*
Priests who, if Satan should sit down,
To make a Bible of his own,
Would gladly for the sake of mitres,
Turn his inspir'd and sacred writers;
Lawyers, who should he wish to prove
His title t' his old seat above,
Would, if his cause he'd give 'em fees in,
Bring writs of *Entry sur disseisin*,
Plead for him boldly at the session,
And hope to put him in possession;   *350*
Merchants who, for his kindly aid,
Would make him partners in their trade,
Hang out their signs in goodly show,
Inscrib'd with *"Belzebub and Co."*
And Judges, who would list his pages,
For proper liveries and wages;
And who as humbly cringe and bow

To all his mortal servants now?
There are; and shame with pointing gestures,
Marks out th' Addressers and Protesters;   360
Whom, following down the stream of fate,
Contempts ineffable await,
And public infamy forlorn,
Dread hate and everlasting scorn."
     As thus he spake, our 'Squire M'Fingal
Gave to his partizans a signal.
Not quicker roll'd the waves to land,
When Moses wav'd his potent wand,
Nor with more uproar, than the Tories
Set up a gen'ral rout in chorus;   370
Laugh'd, hiss'd, hem'd, murmur'd, groan'd and jeer'd;
Honorius now could scarce be heard.
Our Muse amid th' increasing roar,
Could not distinguish one word more:
Tho' she sat by, in firm record
To take in short-hand ev'ry word;
As antient Muses wont, to whom
Old Bards for depositions come;
Who must have writ 'em; for how else
Could they each speech *verbatim* tell 's?   380
And tho' some readers of romances
Are apt to strain their tortur'd fancies,
And doubt, when lovers all alone
Their sad soliloquies do groan,
Grieve many a page with no one near 'em,
And nought but rocks and groves to hear 'em,
What spright infernal could have tattled,
And told the authors all they prattled;
Whence some weak minds have made objection,
That what they scribbled must be fiction: 390
'Tis false; for while the lovers spoke,
The Muse was by, with table-book,

And least some blunder might ensue,
Echo stood clerk and kept the cue.
And tho' the speech ben't worth a groat,
As usual, 'tisn't the author's fault,
But error merely of the prater,
Who should have talk'd to th' purpose better:
Which full excuse, my critic-brothers,
May help me out, as well as others;   *400*
And 'tis design'd, tho' here it lurk,
To serve as preface to this work.
So let it be—for now our 'Squire
No longer could contain his ire;
And rifing 'midst applauding Tories,
Thus vented wrath upon Honorius.
    Quoth he, " 'Tis wondrous what strange stuff
Your Whig's-heads are compounded of;
Which force of logic cannot pierce
Nor syllogistic *carte & tierce,*   *410*
Nor weight of scripture or of reason
Suffice to make the least impression.
Not heeding what ye rais'd contest on,
Ye prate, and beg or steal the question;
And when your boasted arguings fail,
Strait leave all reas'ning off, to rail.
Have not our High-Church Clergy made it
Appear from scriptures which ye credit,
That right divine from heav'n was lent
To kings, that is the Parliament,   *420*
Their subjects to oppress and teaze,
And serve the Devil when they please?
Did they not write and pray and preach,
And torture all the parts of speech,
About Rebellion make a pother,
From one end of the land to th' other?
And yet gain'd fewer pros'lyte Whigs,

Than old *St. Anth'ny 'mongst the pigs;
And chang'd not half so many vicious
As Austin, when he preach'd to fishes;   *430*
Who throng'd to hear, the legend tells,
Were edified and wagg'd their tails:
But scarce you'd prove it, if you tried,
That e'er one Whig was edified.
Have ye not heard from †Parson Walter
Much dire presage of many a halter?
What warnings had ye of your duty
From our old Rev'rend †Sam. Auchmuty?
From Priests of all degrees and metres,
T' our fag-end man poor ‡Parson Peters?   *440*
Have not our Cooper and our Seabury
Sung hymns, like Barak and old Deborah;
Prov'd all intrigues to set you free
Rebellion 'gainst *the pow'rs that be;*
Brought over many a scripture text
That used to wink at rebel sects,
Coax'd wayward ones to favour regents,
Or paraphras'd them to obedience;
Prov'd ev'ry king, ev'n those confest
Horns of th' Apocalyptic beast,   *450*
And sprouting from its noddles seven,
Ordain'd, as bishops are, by heav'n;
(For reasons sim'lar, as we're told
That Tophet was ordain'd of old)

* The stories of St. Anthony and his pig, and St. Austin's preaching to fishes, are told in the Popish legends.
† High-Church Clergymen, one at Boston, one at New-York.
‡ Peters, a Tory-Clergyman in Connecticut, who after making himself detestable by his inimical conduct, absconded from the contempt, rather than the vengeance of his countrymen, and fled to England to make complaints against that colony: Cooper, a writer, poet, and satyrist of the same stamp, President of the college at New-York: Seabury, a Clergyman of the same province.

By this lay-ordination valid
Becomes all sanctified and hallow'd,
Takes patent out when heav'n has sign'd it,
And starts up strait, the Lord's anointed?
Like extreme unction that can cleanse
Each penitent from deadly sins,   *460*
Make them run glib, when oil'd by Priest,
The heav'nly road, like wheels new greas'd,
Serve them, like shoeball, for defences
'Gainst wear and tear of consciences:
So king's anointment cleans betimes,
Like fuller's earth, all spots of crimes,
For future knav'ries gives commissions,
Like Papists sinning under licence.
For heav'n ordain'd the origin,
Divines declare, of pain and sin;   *470*
Prove such great good they both have done us,
Kind mercy 'twas they came upon us:
For without pain and sin and folly
Man ne'er were blest, or wise, or holy;
And we should *thank the Lord, 'tis so,
As authors grave wrote long ago.
Now heav'n its issues never brings
Without the means, and these are kings;
And he, who blames when they announce ills,
Would counteract th' eternal counsels.   *480*
As when the Jews, a murm'ring race,
By constant grumblings fell from grace,
Heav'n taught them first to know their distance
By famine, slav'ry and Philistines;
When these could no repentance bring,
In wrath it sent them last a king:
So nineteen, 'tis believ'd, in twenty

* See the Modern Metaphysical Divinity.

Of modern kings for plagues are sent you;
Nor can your cavillers pretend,
But that they answer well their end.   *490*
'Tis yours to yield to their command, |
As rods in Providence's hand;
And if it means to send you pain,
You turn your noses up in vain;
Your only way's in peace to bear it,
And make necessity a merit.
Hence sure perdition must await
The man, who rises 'gainst the state,
Who meets at once the damning sentence,
Without one loophole for repentance;   *500*
E'en tho' he gain the royal see,
And rank among *the pow'rs that be:*
For hell is theirs, the scripture shows,
Whoe'er *the pow'rs that be* oppose,
And all those pow'rs (I am clear that 'tis so)
Are damn'd for ever, *ex officio.*
    Thus far our Clergy; but 'tis true,
We lack'd not earthly reas'ners too.
Had I the *Poet's brazen lungs
As sound-board to his hundred tongues,   *510*
I could not half the scriblers muster
That swarm'd round Rivington in cluster; |
Assemblies, Councilmen, forsooth;
Brush, Cooper, Wilkins, Chandler, Booth.
Yet all their arguments and sap'ence,
You did not value at three halfpence.
Did not our Massachusettensis†
For your conviction strain his senses?
Scrawl ev'ry moment he could spare,

---

* Virgil's Aeneid, 6th book, line 625.
† See a course of essays, under the signature of Massachusettensis.

From cards and barbers and the fair;   *520*
Show, clear as sun in noonday heavens,
You did not feel a single grievance;
Demonstrate all your opposition
Sprung from the §eggs of foul sedition;
Swear he had seen the nest she laid in,
And knew how long she had been sitting;
Could tell exact what strength of heat is
Requir'd to hatch her out Committees;
What shapes they take, and how much longer's
The space before they grow t' a Congress?   *530*
New whitewash'd Hutchinfon and varnish'd,
Our Gage, who'd got a little tarnish'd,
Made 'em new masks, in time no doubt,
For Hutchinson's was quite worn out;
And while he muddled all his head,
You did not heed a word he said.
Did not our grave †Judge Sewall hit
The summit of news-paper wit?
Fill'd ev'ry leaf of ev'ry paper
Of Mills and Hicks and mother Draper;   *540*
Drew proclamations, works of toil,
In true sublime of scarecrow style;
Wrote farces too, 'gainst Sons of Freedom,
All for your good, and none would read 'em;
Denounc'd damnation on their frenzy,
Who died in Whig-impenitency;
Affirm'd that heav'n would lend us aid,

§ "Committees of Correspondence are the foulest and most venomous serpent, that ever issued from the eggs of sedition," &c.   Massachusettensis.
† Attorney-General of Massachusetts-Bay, a Judge of Admiralty,
Gage's chief Adviser and Proclamation-maker, author of a farce
called the Americans Rouzed, and of a great variety of essays on
the Ministerial side, in the Boston news-papers.

As all our Tory-writers said,
And calculated so its kindness,
He told the moment when it join'd us."   *550*
    " 'Twas then belike, Honorius cried,
When you the public fast defied,
Refus'd to heav'n to raise a prayer,
Because you'd no connections there:
And since with rev'rent hearts and faces
To Governors you'd made addresses,
In them, who made you Tories, seeing
You lived and mov'd and had your being;
Your humble vows you would not breathe
To pow'rs you'd no acquaintance with."   *560*
    "As for your fasts, replied our 'Squire,
What circumstance could fasts require;
We kept them not, but 'twas no crime;
We held them merely loss of time.
For what advantage firm and lasting,
Pray did you ever get by fasting?
And what the gains that can arise
From vows and off'rings to the skies?
Will heav'n reward with posts and fees,
Or send us Tea, as Consignees,   *570*
Give pensions, sal'ries, places, bribes,
Or chuse us judges, clerks, or scribes?
Has it commissions in its gift,
Or cash, to serve us at a lift?
Are acts of parliament there made,
To carry on the placeman's trade?
Or has it pass'd a single bill
To let us plunder whom we will?
And look our list of placemen all over;
Did heav'n appoint our chief judge, Oliver,   *580*
Fill that high bench with ignoramus,
Or has it councils by mandamus?

Who made that wit of *water-gruel,
A Judge of Admiralty, Sewall?
And were they not mere earthly struggles,
That rais'd up Murray, say, and Ruggles?
Did heav'n send down, our pains to med'cine,
That old simplicity of Edson,
Or by election pick out from us,
That Marshfield blund'rer Nat. Ray Thomas;   590
Or had it any hand in serving
A Loring, Pepp'rell, Browne, or Erving?
    Yet we've some saints, the very thing,
We'll pit against the best you'll bring.
For can the strongest fancy paint
Than Hutchinson a greater saint?
Was there a parson used to pray
At times more reg'lar twice a day;
As folks exact have dinners got,
Whether they've appetites or not?   600
Was there a zealot more alarming
'Gainst public vice to hold forth sermon,
Or fix'd at church, whose inward motion
Roll'd up his eyes with more devotion?
What Puritan could ever pray
In Godlier tone, than treas'rer *Gray,
Or at town-meetings speechify'ng,
Could utter more melodious whine,
And shut his eyes and vent his moan,
Like owl afflicted in the sun?   610
Who once sent home his canting rival,
Lord Dartmouth's self, might outbedrivel."
    "Have you forgot, Honorius cried,
How your prime saint the truth defied,
Affirm'd he never wrote a line

* A proper emblem of his genius.
* Treasurer of Massachusetts-Bay, and one of the Mandamus Council.

Your charter'd rights to undermine;
When his own letters then were by,
That prov'd his message all a lie?
How many promises he seal'd,
To get th' oppressive acts repeal'd,   *620*
Yet once arriv'd on England's shore,
Set on the Premier to pass more?
But these are no defects, we grant,
In a right loyal Tory saint,
Whose godlike virtues must with ease
Atone such venal crimes as these:
Or ye perhaps in scripture spy
A new commandment, "Thou shalt lie;"
And if 't be so (as who can tell?)
There's no one sure ye keep so well."   *630*
    "Quoth he, For lies and promise-breaking
Ye need not be in such a taking;
For lying is, we know and teach,
The highest privilege of speech;
The universal Magna Charta,
To which all human race is party,
Whence children first, as David says,
Lay claim to 't in their earliest days;
The only stratagem in war,
Our Gen'rals have occasion for;   *640*
The only freedom of the press
Our politicians need in peace:
And 'tis a shame you wish t' abridge us
Of these our darling privileges.
Thank heav'n, your shot have miss'd their aim,
For lying is no sin, or shame.
    As men last wills may change again,
Tho' drawn in name of God, amen;
Be sure they must have much the more,
O'er promises as great a pow'r,   *650*

Which made in haste, with small inspection,
So much the more will need correction;
And when they've careless spoke, or penn'd 'em,
Have right to look 'em o'er and mend 'em;
Revise their vows, or change the text,
By way of codicil annex'd,
Turn out a promise, that was base,
And put a better in its place.
So Gage of late agreed, you know,
To let the Boston people go;   660
Yet when he saw 'gainst troops that brav'd him,
They were the only guards that sav'd him,
Kept off that Satan of a Putnam,
From breaking in to maul and mutt'n him;
He'd too much wit such leagues t' observe,
And shut them in again to starve.
   So Moses writes, when female Jews
Made oaths and vows unfit for use,
Their parents then might set them free
From that conscientious tyranny: 670
And shall men feel that spir'tual bondage
Forever, when they grow beyond age;
Nor have pow'r their own oaths to change?
I think the tale were very strange.
Shall vows but bind the stout and strong,
And let go women weak and young,
As nets enclose the larger crew,
And let the smaller fry creep thro'?
Besides, the Whigs have all been set on,
The Tories to affright and threaten,   680
Till Gage amidst his trembling fits
Has hardly kept him in his wits;
And tho' he speak with art and finesse,
'Tis said beneath *duress per minas.*
For we're in peril of our souls

From feathers, tar and lib'rty-poles:
And vows extorted are not binding
In law, and so not worth the minding.
For we have in this hurly-burly
Sent off our consciences on furlow, 690
Thrown our religion o'er in form;
Our ship to lighten in the storm.
Nor need we blush your Whigs before;
If we've no virtue you've no more.
    Yet black with sins, would stain a mitre,
Rail ye at crimes by ten tints whiter,
And stuff'd with choler atrabilious,
Insult us here for peccadilloes?
While all your vices run so high
That mercy scarce could find supply: 700
While should you offer to repent,
You'd need more fasting days than Lent,
More groans than haunted churchyard vallies,
And more confessions than broad-alleys.
I'll show you all at fitter time,
The extent and greatness of your crime,
And here demonstrate to your face,
Your want of virtue, as of grace,
Evinced from topics old and recent:
But thus much must suffice at present. 710
To th' after-portion of the day,
I leave what more remains to say;
When I've good hope you'll all appear,
More fitted and prepared to hear,
And griev'd for all your vile demeanour:
But now 'tis time t' adjourn for dinner."

The

Town Meeting

P.M.

THE SUN, who never stops to dine,
Two hours had pass'd the midway line,
And driving at his usual rate,
Lash'd on his downward car of state.
And now expired the short vacation,
And dinner done in epic fashion;
While all the crew beneath the trees,
Eat pocket-pies, or bread and cheese;
Nor shall we, like old Homer care
To versify their bill of fare.   *10*
For now each party, feasted well,
Throng'd in, like sheep, at sound of bell,
With equal spirit took their places;
And meeting oped with three Oh yesses:
When first the daring Whigs t' oppose,
Again the great M'Fingal rose,

Stretch'd magisterial arm amain,
And thus assum'd th' accusing strain.
   "Ye Whigs attend, and hear affrighted
The crimes whereof ye stand indicted, 20
The sins and follies past all compass,
That prove you guilty or non compos.
I leave the verdict to your senses,
And jury of your consciences;
Which tho' they're neither good nor true,
Must yet convict you and your crew.
Ungrateful sons! a factious band,
That rise against your parent-land!
Ye viper'd race, that burst in strife,
The welcome womb, that gave you life, 30
Tear with sharp fangs and forked tongue,
Th' indulgent bowels, whence you sprung;
And scorn the debt of obligation
You justly owe the British nation,
Which since you cannot pay, your crew
Affect to swear 'twas never due.
Did not the deeds of England's Primate
First drive your fathers to this climate,
Whom jails and fines and ev'ry ill
Forc'd to their good against their will? 40
Ye owe to their obliging temper
The peopling your newfangled empire,
While ev'ry British act and canon
Stood forth your *causa sine qua non.*
Did they not send you charters o'er,
And give you lands you own'd before,
Permit you all to spill your blood,
And drive out heathen where you could;
On these mild terms, that conquest won,
The realm you gain'd should be their own. 50
Or when of late attack'd by those,

Whom her connection made your foes,
Did they not then, distrest in war,
Send Gen'rals to your help from far,
Whose aid you own'd in terms less haughty,
And thankfully o'erpaid your quota?
Say, at what period did they grudge
To send you Governor or Judge,
With all their missionary crew,
To teach you law and gospel too?   60
Brought o'er all felons in the nation,
To help you on in population;
Propos'd their Bishops to surrender
And made their Priests a legal tender,
Who only ask'd in surplice clad,
The simple tythe of all you had:
And now to keep all knaves in awe,
Have sent their troops t' establish law,
And with gunpowder, fire and ball,
Reform your people one and all.   70
Yet when their insolence and pride
Have anger'd all the world beside,
When fear and want at once invade,
Can you refuse to lend them aid;
And rather risque your heads in fight,
Than gratefully throw in your mite?
Can they for debts make satisfaction,
Should they dispose their realm by auction;
And sell off Britain's goods and land all
To France and Spain by inch of candle?   80
Shall good king George, with want opprest,
Insert his name in bankrupt list,
And shut up shop, like failing merchant,
That fears the bailiffs should make search in't;
With poverty shall princes strive,
And nobles lack whereon to live?

Have they not rack'd their whole inventions,
To feed their brats on posts and pensions,
Made ev'n Scotch friends with taxes groan,
And pick'd poor Ireland to the bone;   *90*
Yet have on hand as well deserving,
Ten thousand bastards left for starving?
And can you now with conscience clear,
Refuse them an asylum here,
Or not maintain in manner fitting,
These genuine sons of mother Britain?
T' evade these crimes of blackest grain,
You prate of liberty in vain,
And strive to hide your vile designs,
With terms abstruse like school-divines.   *100*
 Your boasted patriotism is scarce,
And country's love is but a farce;
And after all the proofs you bring,
We Tories know there's no such thing.
Our English writers of great fame
Prove public virtue but a name.
Hath not *Dalrymple show'd in print,
And *Johnson too, there's nothing in't?
Produc'd you demonstration ample
From other's and their own example,   *110*
That self is still, in either faction,
The only principle of action;
The loadstone, whose attracting tether
Keeps the politic world together:
And spite of all your double-dealing,
We Tories know 'tis so, by feeling.
 Who heeds your babbling of transmitting
Freedom to brats of your begetting,
Or will proceed as though there were a tie,

* Ministerial Pensioners.

Or obligation to posterity?   *120*
We get 'em, bear 'em, breed and nurse;
What has poster'ty done for us,
That we, lest they their rights should lose,
Should trust our necks to gripe of noose?
   And who believes you will not run?
You're cowards, ev'ry mother's son;
And should you offer to deny,
We've witnesses to prove it by.
Attend th' opinion first, as referee,
Of your old Gen'ral, stout Sir Jeffery,   *130*
Who swore that with five thousand foot
He'd rout you all, and in pursuit,
Run thro' the land as easily,
As camel thro' a needle's eye.
Did not the valiant Col'nel Grant
Against your courage make his slant,
Affirm your universal failure
In ev'ry principle of valour,
And swear no scamp'rers e'er could match you,
So swift, a bullet scarce could catch you?   *140*
And will ye not confess in this,
A judge most competent he is,
Well skill'd on runnings to decide,
As what himself has often tried?
'Twould not methinks be labour lost,
If you'd sit down and count the cost;
And ere you call your Yankies out,
First think what work you've set about.
Have ye not rouz'd, his force to try on,
That grim old beast, the British lion?   *150*
And know you not that at a sup
He's large enough to eat you up?
Have you survey'd his jaws beneath,
Drawn inventories of his teeth,

Or have you weigh'd in even balance
His strength and magnitude of talons?
His roar would turn your boasts to fear,
As easily as sour small-beer,
And make your feet from dreadful fray,
By native instinct run away.   *160*
Britain, depend on't, will take on her
T' assert her dignity and honor,
And ere she'd lose your share of pelf,
Destroy your country and herself.
For has not North declar'd they fight
To gain substantial rev'nue by't,
Denied he'd ever deign to treat,
Till on your knees and at his feet?
And feel you not a trifling ague,
From Van's *Delenda est Carthago?*   *170*
For this, now Britain has come to't,
Think you she has not means to do't?
Has she not set to work all engines
To spirit up the native Indians,
Send on your backs a savage band,
With each a hatchet in his hand,
T' amuse themselves with scalping knives,
And butcher children and your wives;
That she may boast again with vanity,
Her English national humanity?   *180*
(For now in its primaeval sense,
This term, *human'ty,* comprehends
All things of which, on this side hell,
The *human mind* is capable;
And thus 'tis well, by writers sage,
Applied to Britain and to Gage.)
And on this work to raise allies,
She sent her duplicate of Guys,
To drive, at diff'rent parts at once, on

Her stout Guy Carlton and Guy Johnson: *190*
To each of whom, to send again ye
Old Guy of Warwick were a ninny;
Tho' the dun cow he fell'd in war,
These killcows are his betters far.
   And has she not assay'd her notes,
To rouze your slaves to cut your throats,
Sent o'er ambassadors with guineas,
To bribe your blacks in Carolinas?
And has not Gage, her missionary
Turn'd many an Afric slave t' a Tory,   *200*
And made th' Amer'can bishop's see grow,
By many a new-converted Negro?
As friends to gov'rnment did not he
Their slaves at Boston late set free;
Enlist them all in black parade,
Set off with regimental red?
And were they not accounted then
Among his very bravest men?
And when such means she stoops to take,
Think you she is not wide awake?   *210*
As Eliphaz' good man in Job
Own'd num'rous allies thro' the globe;
Had brought the *stones along the street
To ratify a cov'nant meet,
And ev'ry beast from lice to lions,
To join in leagues of strict alliance:
Has she not cring'd, in spite of pride,
For like assistance far and wide?
Was there a creature so despis'd,

* The stones and all the elements with thee
Shall ratify a strict confed'racy;
Wild beasts their savage temper shall forget,
And for a firm alliance with thee treat: &c.
                Blackmore's Paraphrase of Job.

Its aid she has not sought and priz'd? 220
Till all this formidable league rose
Of Indians, British troops and Negroes,
And can you break these triple bands
By all your workmanship of hands?"
   "Sir, quoth Honorius, we presume
You guess from past feats, what's to come,
And from the mighty deeds of Gage,
Foretell how fierce the war he'll wage.
You doubtless recollected here
The annals of his first great year: 230
While wearying out the Tories' patience,
He spent his breath in proclamations;
While all his mighty noise and vapour
Was used in wrangling upon paper;
And boasted military fits
Closed in the straining of his wits;
While troops in Boston commons plac'd
Laid nought but quires of paper waste;
While strokes alternate stunn'd the nation,
Protest, address and proclamation; 240
And speech met speech, fib clash'd with fib,
And Gage still answer'd, squib for squib.
   Tho' this not all his time was lost on;
He fortified the town of Boston;
Built breastworks that might lend assistance
To keep the patriots at a distance;
(For howsoe'er the rogues might scoff,
He liked them best the farthest off)
Of mighty use and help to aid
His courage, when he felt afraid; 250
And whence right off in manful station,
He'd boldly pop his proclamation.
Our hearts must in our bosoms freeze
At such heroic deeds as these."

"Vain, quoth the 'Squire, you'll find to sneer
At Gage's first triumphant year;
For Providence, dispos'd to teaze us,
Can use what instruments it pleases.
To pay a tax at Peter's wish,
His chief cashier was once a Fish;   260
An Ass, in Balaam's sad disaster,
Turn'd orator and sav'd his master;
A Goose plac'd centry on his station
Preserv'd old Rome from desolation;
An English Bishop's *Cur of late
Disclosed rebellions 'gainst the state;
So Frogs croak'd Pharaoh to repentance,
And Lice revers'd the threat'ning sentence:
And heav'n can ruin you at pleasure,
By our scorn'd Gage, as well as Caesar.   270
Yet did our hero in these days
Pick up some laurel wreaths of praise.
And as the statuary of Seville
Made his crackt saint an exc'llent devil;
So tho' our war few triumphs brings,
We gain'd great fame in other things.
Did not our troops show much discerning,
And skill your various arts in learning?
Outwent they not each native Noodle
By far in playing Yanky-doodle;   280
Which, as 'twas your New-England tune,
'Twas marvellous they took so soon?
And ere the year was fully thro',
Did not they learn to foot it too;
And such a dance as ne'er was known,
For twenty miles on end lead down?
Was there a Yanky trick you knew,

* See Bishop Atterbury's trial.

They did not play as well as you?
Did they not lay their heads together,
And gain your art to tar and feather,   *290*
When Col'nel Nesbitt thro' the town,
In triumph bore the country-clown?
Oh, what a glorious work to sing
The vet'ran troops of Britain's king,
Advent'ring for th'heroic laurel,
With bag of feathers and tar-barrel!
To paint the cart where culprits ride,
And Nesbitt marching at its side,
Great executioner and proud,
Like hangman high on Holbourn road;   *300*
And o'er the bright triumphal car
The waving ensigns of the war!
As when a triumph Rome decreed,
For great Calig'la's valiant deed,
Who had subdued the British seas,
By gath'ring cockles from their base;
In pompous car the conqu'ror bore
His captiv'd scallops from the shore,
Ovations gain'd his crabs for fetching,
And mighty feats of oyster-catching: *310*
O'er Yankies thus the war begun,
They tarr'd and triumph'd over one;
And fought and boasted thro' the season,
With might as great, and equal reason.
    Yet thus, tho' skill'd in vict'ry's toils,
They boast, not unexpert, in wiles.
For gain'd they not an equal fame in
The arts of secrecy and scheming?
In stratagems show'd mighty force,
And moderniz'd the Trojan horse,   *320*
Play'd o'er again those trick Ulyssean,
In their fam'd Salem-expedition?

For as that horse, the Poets tell ye,
Bore Grecian armies in his belly;
Till their full reck'ning run, with joy
Their Sinon midwif'd them in Troy:
So in one ship was Leslie bold
Cramm'd with three hundred men in hold,
Equipp'd for enterprize and sail,
Like Jonas stow'd in womb of whale.   *330*
To Marblehead in depth of night,
The cautious vessel wing'd her flight.
And now the sabbath's silent day
Call'd all your Yankies off to pray;
Remov'd each prying jealous neighbour,
The scheme and vessel fell in labour;
Forth from its hollow womb pour'd hast'ly
The Myrmidons of Col'nel Leslie:
Not thicker o'er the blacken'd strand
The *frogs' detachment rush'd to land,   *340*
Equipp'd by onset or surprize
To storm th' entrenchment of the mice.
Thro' Salem strait without delay,
The bold battalion took its way,
March'd o'er a bridge in open sight
Of sev'ral Yankies arm'd for fight,
Then without loss of time, or men
Veer'd round for Boston back again;
And found so well their projects thrive,
That ev'ry soul got home alive.   *350*
    Thus Gage's arms did fortune bless
With triumph, safety and success:
But mercy is without dispute
His first and darling attribute;
So great it far outwent and conquer'd

* See Homer's battle of the frogs and mice.

His military skill at Concord.
There when the war he chose to wage
Shone the benevolence of Gage;
Sent troops to that ill-omen'd place
On errands meer of special grace,   *360*
And all the work he chose them for
Was to †prevent a civil war:
And for that purpose he projected
The only certain way t' effect it,
To take your powder, stores and arms,
And all your means of doing harms:
As prudent folks take knives away,
Lest children cut themselves at play.
And yet tho' this was all his scheme,
This war you still will charge on him;   *370*
And tho' he oft has swore and said it,
Stick close to facts and give no credit.
Think you, he wish'd you'd brave and beard him?
Why, 'twas the very thing that scar'd him.
He'd rather you should all have run,
Than stay'd to fire a single gun.
And for the civil war you lament,
Faith, you yourselves must take the blame in't;
For had you then, as he intended,
Giv'n up your arms, it must have ended.   *380*
Since that's no war, each mortal knows,
Where one side only gives the blows,
And th' other bears 'em; on reflection
The most you'll call it is correction.
Nor could the contest have gone higher,
If you had ne'er return'd the fire;
But when you shot, and not before,
It then commenc'd a civil war.

† See Gage's answer to Governor Trumbull.

Else Gage, to end this controversy,
Had but corrected you in mercy: *390*
Whom mother Britain old and wise,
Sent o'er, the Col'nies to chastise;
Command obedience on their peril
Of ministerial whip and ferule;
And since they ne'er must come of age,
Govern'd and tutor'd them by Gage.
Still more, that this was all their errand,
The army's conduct makes apparent.
What tho' at Lexington you can say
They kill'd a few they did not fancy,   *400*
At Concord then, with manful popping,
Discharg'd a round the ball to open?
Yet when they saw your rebel-rout
Determin'd still to hold it out;
Did they not show their love to peace,
And wish, that discord strait might cease,
Demonstrate, and by proofs uncommon,
Their orders were to injure no man?
For did not ev'ry Reg'lar run
As soon as e'er you fir'd a gun;   *410*
Take the first shot you sent them greeting,
As meant their signal for retreating;
And fearful if they staid for sport,
You might by accident be hurt,
Convey themselves with speed away
Full twenty miles in half a day;
Race till their legs were grown so weary,
They'd scarce suffice their weight to carry?
Whence Gage extols, from gen'ral hearsay,
The great *activ'ty of Lord Piercy;   *420*

* "Too much praise cannot be given to Lord Percy for his remarkable activity thro' the whole day." *Gage's account of the Lexington battle.*

Whose brave example led them on,
And spirited the troops to run;
And now may boast at royal levees
A Yanky-chace worth forty Chevys.
Yet you as vile as they were kind,
Pursued, like tygers, still behind,
Fir'd on them at your will, and shut
The town, as tho' you'd starve them out;
And with †parade prepost'rous hedg'd
Affect to hold them there besieg'd;   *430*
(Tho' Gage, whom proclamations call
Your Gov'rnor and Vice-Admiral,
Whose pow'r gubernatorial still
Extends as far as Bunker's hill;
Whose admiralty reaches clever,
Near half a mile up Mystic river,
Whose naval force commands the seas,
Can run away when'er he please)
Scar'd troops of Tories into town,
And burnt their hay and houses down,   *440*
And menac'd Gage, unless he'd flee,
To drive him headlong to the sea;
As once, to faithless Jews a sign,
The de'el, turn'd hog-reeve, did the swine.
   But now your triumphs all are o'er;
For see from Britain's angry shore
With mighty hosts of valour join
Her Howe, her Clinton and Burgoyne.
As comets thro' the affrighted skies
Pour baleful ruin, as they rise;   *450*
As Aetna with infernal roar
In conflagration sweeps the shore;

† "And with a preposterous parade of military arrangement they affect to hold the army besieged." *Gage's last grand proclamation.*

Or as *Abijah White when sent
Our Marshfield friends to represent,
Himself while dread array involves,
Commissions, pistols, swords, resolves,
In awful pomp descending down,
Bore terror on the factious town:
Not with less glory and affright,
Parade these Gen'rals forth to fight.   460
No more each Reg'lar †Col'nel runs
From whizzing beetles, as air-guns,
Thinks hornbugs bullets, or thro' fears
Muskitoes takes for musketeers;
Nor 'scapes, as tho' you'd gain'd allies
From Belzebub's whole host of flies.
No bug their warlike hearts appalls;
They better know the sound of balls.
I hear the din of battle bray,
The trump of horror marks its way.   470
I see afar the sack of cities,
The gallows strung with Whig-committees;
Your Moderators triced, like vermin,
And gate-posts graced with heads of Chairmen;
Your Gen'rals for wave-offrings hanging,
And ladders throng'd with Priests haranguing.
What pill'ries glad the Tories' eyes

* He was a representative of Marshfield, and employed to carry their famous town-resolves to Boston. He armed himself in as ridiculous military array, as another Hudibras, pretending he was afraid he should be robb'd of them.

† This was a fact. Some British officers, soon after Gage's arrival in Boston, walking on Beacon-Hill after sunset, were affrighted by noises in the air (supposed to be the flying of bugs and beetles) which they took to be the sound of bullets, and left the hill with great precipitation: Concerning which they wrote terrible accounts to England of their being shot at with air-guns; as appears by one or two letters, extracts from which were published in the English papers.

With patriot-ears for sacrifice!
What whipping-posts your chosen race
Admit successive in embrace,   *480*
While each bears off his crimes, alack!
Like Bunyan's pilgrim, on his back!
Where then, when Tories scarce get clear,
Shall Whigs and Congresses appear?
What rocks and mountains shall you call
To wrap you over with their fall,
And save your heads in these sad weathers,
From fire and sword, and tar and feathers!
For lo, with British troops tarbright,
Again our Nesbitt heaves in sight!   *490*
He comes, he comes, your lines to storm,
And rigg your troops in uniform!
To meet such heroes, will ye brag,
With fury arm'd, and feather-bag;
Who wield their missile pitch and tar,
With engines new in British war?
    Lo, where our mighty navy brings
Destruction on her canvas-wings,
While thro' the deeps her potent thunder
Shall sound th' alarm to rob and plunder!   *500*
As Phoebus first, so Homer speaks,
When he march'd out t' attack the Greeks,
'Gainst mules sent forth his arrows fatal,
And slew th' auxiliaries, their cattle;
So where our ships shall stretch the keel,
What conquer'd oxen shall they steal!
What heroes rising from the deep
Invade your marshall'd hosts of sheep!
Disperse whole troops of horse, and pressing,
Make cows surrender at discretion;   *510*
Attack your hens, like Alexanders,
And reg'ments rout of geese and ganders;

Or where united arms combine
Lead captive many a herd of swine!
Then rush in dreadful fury down
To fire on ev'ry seaport town;
Display their glory and their wits,
Fright unarm'd children into fits,
And stoutly from th' unequal fray,
Make many a woman run away!   *520*
And can ye doubt whene'er we please
Our chiefs shall boast such deeds as these?
Have we not chiefs transcending far,
The old fam'd *thunderbolts of war;*
Beyond the brave romantic fighters,
Stiled *swords of death by* novel-writers?
Nor in romancing ages e'er rose
So terrible a tier of heroes.
From Gage, what flashes fright the waves!
How loud a blunderbuss is Graves!   *530*
How Newport dreads the blustring sallies,
That thunder from our popgun, Wallace,
While noise in formidable strains
Spouts from his thimble-full of brains!
I see you sink with aw'd surprize!
I see our Tory-brethren rise!
And as the sect'ries Sandemanian,
Our friends describe their wish'd Millennium;
Tell how the world in ev'ry region
At once shall own their true religion;   *540*
For heav'n with plagues of awful dread
Shall knock all heretics o' th' head;
And then their church, the meek in spirit,
The earth, as promis'd, shall inherit,
From the dead wicked, as heirs male,
And next remainder-men in tail:
Such ruin shall the Whigs oppress!

Such spoils our Tory friends shall bless!
While Confiscation at command
Shall stalk in horror thro' the land,   *550*
Shall give your Whig-estates away,
And call our brethren into play.
    And can ye doubt or scruple more,
These things are near you at the door?
Behold! for tho' to reas'ning blind,
Signs of the times ye sure might mind,
And view impending fate as plain
As ye'd foretell a show'r of rain.
    Hath not heav'n warn'd you what must ensue,
And Providence declar'd against you;   *560*
Hung forth its dire portents of war,
By *signs and beacons in the air;
Alarm'd old women all around
By fearful noises under ground;
While earth for many dozen leagues
Groan'd with her dismal load of Whigs?
Was there a meteor far and wide
But muster'd on the Tory-side?
A star malign that has not bent
Its aspects for the Parliament,   *570*
Foreboding your defeat and misery;
As once they fought against old Sisera?
Was there a cloud that spread the skies,
But bore our armies of allies?
While dreadful hosts of fire stood forth
'Mid baleful glimm'rings from the North;
Which plainly shows which part they join'd,
For North's the minister, ye mind;

* Such stories of prodigies were at that time industriously propagated by the Tory-party in various parts of New-England, to terrify and intimidate the superstitious.

Whence oft your quibblers in gazettes
On *Northern blasts* have strain'd their wits;   *580*
And think ye not the clouds know how
To make the pun as well as you?
Did there arise an apparition,
But grinn'd forth ruin to sedition?
A death-watch, but has join'd our leagues,
And click'd destruction to the Whigs?
Heard ye not, when the wind was fair,
At night our or'tors in the air,
That, loud as admiralty-libel,
Read awful chapters from the bible,   *590*
And death and deviltry denounc'd,
And told you how you'd soon be trounc'd?
I see to join our conqu'ring side
Heav'n, earth and hell at once allied!
See from your overthrow and end
The Tories paradise ascend;
Like that new world that claims its station
Beyond the final conflagration!
I see the day that lots your share
In utter darkness and despair;   *600*
The day of joy, when North, our Lord,
His faithful fav'rites shall reward!
No Tory then shall set before him
Small wish of 'Squire, or Justice Quorum;
But 'fore his unmistaken eyes
See Lordships, posts and pensions rise.
Awake to gladness then, ye Tories,
Th' unbounded prospect lies before us?
The pow'r display'd in Gage's banners
Shall cut Amer'can lands to manors,   *610*
And o'er our happy conquer'd ground
Dispense estates and titles round.
Behold, the world shall stare at new setts

Of home-made *earls in Massachusetts;
Admire, array'd in ducal tassels,
Your Ol'vers, Hutchinsons and Vassals;
See join'd in ministerial work
His grace of Albany and York!
What Lordships from each carv'd estate,
On our New-York Assembly wait!　　　　　　　　*620*
What titled †Jauncys, Gales and Billops;
Lord Brush, Lord Wilkins and Lord Philips!
In wide-sleev'd pomp of godly guise,
What solemn rows of bishops rise!
Aloft a card'nal's hat is spread
O'er punster §Cooper's rev'rend head!
In Vardell, that poetic zealot,
I view a lawn-bedizen'd prelate!
While mitres fall, as 'tis their duty,
On heads of Chandler and Auchmuty!　　　　　　*630*
Knights, viscounts, barons shall ye meet,
As thick as pavements in the street!
Ev'n I perhaps, heav'n speed my claim,
Shall fix a *Sir* before my name.
For titles all our foreheads ache;
For what blest changes can they make!
Place rev'rence, grace and excellence
Where neither claim'd the least pretence;
Transform by patent's magic words
Men, likest devils, into Lords;　　　　　　　　*640*
Whence commoners to peers translated
Are justly said to be *created!*

* See Hutchinson's and Oliver's letters.
† Members of the ministerial Majority in the New-York assembly;
Wilkins a noted writer.
§ President Cooper is a notorious punster: Vardell, author of some
poetical satires on the sons of liberty in New-York, and royal pro-
fessor in King's college; Chandler and Auchmuty, High-church and
Tory-writers of the Clerical order.

Now where commissioners ye saw
Shall boards of nobles deal you law!
Long-rob'd comptrollers judge your rights,
And tide-waiters start up in knights!
While Whigs subdued in slavish awe,
Our wood shall hew, our water draw,
And bless that mildness, when past hope,
Which sav'd their necks from noose of rope.   *650*
For as to gain assistance we
Design their Negroes to set free;
For Whigs, when we enough shall bang 'em,
Perhaps 'tis better not to hang 'em;
Except their chiefs; the vulgar knaves
Will do more good preserv'd for slaves."
     " 'Tis well, Honorius cried, your scheme
Has painted out a pretty dream.
We can't confute your second sight;
We shall be slaves and you a knight: *660*
These things must come: but I divine
They'll come not in your day, or mine.
But oh, my friends, my brethren, hear,
And turn for once th' attentive ear.
Ye see how prompt to aid our woes,
The tender mercies of our foes;
Ye see with what unvaried rancour
Still for our blood their minions hanker,
Nor aught can sate their mad ambition,
From us, but death, or worse, submission.   *670*
Shall these then riot in our spoil,
Reap the glad harvest of our toil,
Rise from their country's ruin proud,
And roll their chariot wheels in blood?
And can ye sleep while high outspread
Hangs desolation o'er your head?
See Gage with inauspicious star

Has oped the gates of civil war;
When streams of gore from freemen slain,
Encrimson'd Concord's fatal plain;   *680*
Whose warning voice with awful sound,
Still cries, like Abel's from the ground,
And heav'n, attentive to its call,
Shall doom the proud oppressor's fall.
    Rise then, ere ruin swift surprize,
To victory, to vengeance rise!
Hark, how the distant din alarms!
The echoing trumpet breathes, to arms:
From provinces remote, afar,
The sons of glory rouze to war;   *690*
'Tis freedom calls; th' enraptur'd sound
The Apalachian hills rebound;
The Georgian shores her voice shall hear,
And start from lethargies of fear.
From the parch'd zone, with glowing ray,
Where pours the sun intenser day,
To shores where icy waters roll,
And tremble to the dusky pole,
Inspir'd by freedom's heav'nly charms,
United nations wake to arms.   *700*
The star of conquest lights their way,
And guides their vengeance on their prey—
Yes, tho' tyrannic force oppose,
Still shall they triumph o'er their foes,
Till heav'n the happy land shall bless,
With safety, liberty and peace.
    And ye whose souls of dastard mould
Start at the brav'ry of the bold;
To love your country who pretend,
Yet want all spirit to defend;   *710*
Who feel your fancies so prolific,
Engend'ring vision'd whims terrific,

O'er-run with horrors of coercion,
Fire, blood and thunder in reversion,
King's standards, pill'ries, confiscations,
And Gage's scarecrow proclamations,
With all the trumpery of fear;
Hear bullets whizzing in your rear;
Who scarce could rouze, if caught in fray,
Presence of mind to run away;   720
See nought but halters rise to view
In all your dreams (and dreams are true)
And while these phantoms haunt your brains,
Bow down the willing neck to chains;
Heav'ns! are ye sons of sires so great,
Immortal in the fields of fate,
Who brav'd all deaths by land or sea,
Who bled, who conquer'd to be free!
Hence, coward souls, the worst disgrace
Of our forefathers' valiant race;   730
Hie homeward from the glorious field;
There turn the wheel, the distaff wield;
Act what ye are, nor dare to stain
The warrior's arms with touch profane:
There beg your more heroic wives
To guard your children and your lives;
Beneath their aprons find a screen,
Nor dare to mingle more with men."
    As thus he said, the Tories' anger
Could now restrain itself no longer,   740
Who tried before by many a freak, or
Insulting noise, to stop the speaker;
Swung th' unoil'd hinge of each pew-door;
Their feet kept shuffling on the floor;
Made their disapprobation known
By many a murmur, hum and groan,
That to his speech supplied the place

Of counterpart in thorough-base:
As bag-pipes, while the tune they breathe,
Still drone and grumble underneath;   *750*
Or as the fam'd Demosthenes
Harangued the rumbling of the seas,
Held forth with eloquence full grave
To audience loud of wind and wave;
And had a stiller congregation
Than Tories are to hear th' oration.
But now the storm grew high and louder
As nearer thundrings of a cloud are,
And ev'ry soul with heart and voice
Supplied his quota of the noise;   *760*
Each listning ear was set on torture
Each Tory bell'wing out, to order;
And some, with tongue not low or weak,
Were clam'ring fast, for leave to speak;
The moderator, with great vi'lence,
The cushion thump'd with "Silence, silence;"
The constable to ev'ry prater
Bawl'd out, "Pray hear the moderator;"
Some call'd the vote, and some in turn
Were screaming high, "Adjourn, adjourn:"   *770*
Not chaos heard such jars and clashes
When all the el'ments fought for places.
Each bludgeon soon for blows was tim'd;
Each fist stood ready cock'd and prim'd;
The storm each moment louder grew;
His sword the great M'Fingal drew,
Prepar'd in either chance to share,
To keep the peace, or aid the war.
Nor lack'd they each poetic being,
Whom bards alone are skill'd in seeing;   *780*
Plum'd Victory stood perch'd on high,
Upon the pulpit-canopy,

To join, as is her custom tried,
Like Indians, on the strongest side;
The Destinies with shears and distaff,
Drew near their threads of life to twist off;
The Furies 'gan to feast on blows,
And broken heads or bloody nose;
When on a sudden from without
Arose a loud terrific shout;   *790*
And strait the people all at once heard
Of tongues an universal concert;
Like Aesop's times, as fable runs,
When ev'ry creature talk'd at once,
Or like the variegated gabble
That craz'd the carpenters of Babel.
Each party soon forgot the quarrel,
And let the other go on parole;
Eager to know what fearful matter
Had conjur'd up such gen'ral clatter;   *800*
And left the church in thin array,
As tho' it had been lecture-day.
Our 'Squire M'Fingal straitway beckon'd
The constable to stand his second,
And sallied forth with aspect fierce
The croud assembled to disperse.
The moderator out of view
Beneath a bench had lain perdue;
Peep'd up his head to view the fray,
Beheld the wranglers run away,   *810*
And left alone with solemn face,
Adjourn'd them without time or place.

The

Liberty Pole

NOW ARM'D with ministerial ire,
Fierce sallied forth our loyal 'Squire,
And on his striding steps attends,
His desp'rate clan of Tory friends;
When sudden met his angry eye,
A pole, ascending thro' the sky,
Which num'rous throngs of Whiggish race
Were raising in the market-place;
Not higher school-boys kites aspire,
Or royal mast or country spire,   10
Like spears at Brobdignagian tilting,
Or Satan's walking-staff in Milton;
And on its top the flag unfurl'd,
Waved triumph o'er the prostrate world,
Inscribed with inconsistent types
Of liberty and thirteen stripes.

Beneath, the croud without delay,
The dedication-rites essay,
And gladly pay in antient fashion,
The ceremonies of libation;   20
While briskly to each patriot lip
Walks eager round th' inspiring flip:
Delicious draught, whose pow'rs inherit
The quintessence of public spirit!
Which whoso tastes, perceives his mind
To nobler politics refined,
Or rouz'd for martial controversy,
As from transforming cups of Circe;
Or warm'd with Homer's nectar'd liquor,
That fill'd the veins of gods with ichor.   30
At hand for new supplies in store,
The tavern opes its friendly door,
Whence to and fro the waiters run,
Like bucket-men at fires in town.
Then with three shouts that tore the sky,
'Tis consecrate to Liberty;
To guard it from th' attacks of Tories,
A grand committee cull'd of four is,
Who foremost on the patriot spot,
Had brought the flip and paid the shot.   40
    By this, M'Fingal with his train,
Advanc'd upon th' adjacent plain,
And fierce with loyal rage possess'd,
Pour'd forth the zeal, that fired his breast.
"What madbrain'd rebel gave commission,
To raise this Maypole of sedition!
Like Babel rear'd by bawling throngs,
With like confusion too of tongues,
To point at heav'n and summon down,
The thunders of the British crown?   50
Say will this paltry pole secure

Your forfeit heads from Gage's pow'r?
Attack'd by heroes brave and crafty,
Is this to stand your ark of safety?
Or driv'n by Scottish laird and laddie,
Think ye to rest beneath its shadow?
When bombs, like fiery serpents, fly
And balls move hissing thro'the sky,
With this vile pole, devote to freedom,
Save like the Jewish pole in Edom,   *60*
Or like the brazen snake of Moses,
Cure your crackt skulls and batter'd noses?
Ye dupes to ev'ry factious rogue,
Or tavernprating demagogue,
Whose tongue but rings, with sound more full,
On th' empty drumhead of his skull,
Behold you know not what noisy fools
Use you, worse simpletons, for tools?
For Liberty in your own by-sense
Is but for crimes a patent licence;   *70*
To break of law th' Egyptian yoke,
And throw the world in common stock,
Reduce all grievances and ills
To Magna Charta of your wills,
Establish cheats and frauds and nonsense,
Fram'd by the model of your conscience,
Cry justice down, as out of fashion
And fix its scale of depreciation,
Defy all creditors to trouble ye,
And pass new years of Jewish jubilee;   *80*
Drive judges out, like Aaron's calves,
By jurisdictions of white staves,
And make the bar and bench and steeple,
Submit t' our sov'reign Lord, the People;
Assure each knave his whole assets,
By gen'ral amnesty of debts;

By plunder rise to pow'r and glory,
And brand all property as tory;
Expose all wares to lawful seizures
Of mobbers and monopolizers;   *90*
Break heads and windows and the peace,
For your own int'rest and increase;
Dispute and pray and fight and groan,
For public good, and mean your own;
Prevent the laws, by fierce attacks,
From quitting scores upon your backs,
Lay your old dread, the gallows, low,
And seize the stocks your antient foe;
And turn them, as convenient engines
To wreak your patriotic vengeance;   *100*
While all, your claims who understand,
Confess they're in the owner's hand:
And when by clamours and confusions,
Your freedom's grown a public nuisance,
Cry, Liberty, with pow'rful yearning,
As he does, fire, whose house is burning,
Tho' he already has much more,
Than he can find occasion for.
While ev'ry dunce, that turns the plains
Tho' bankrupt in estate and brains,   *110*
By this new light transform'd to traitor,
Forsakes his plow to turn dictator,
Starts an haranguing chief of Whigs,
And drags you by the ears, like pigs.
All bluster arm'd with factious licence,
Transform'd at once to politicians;
Each leather-apron'd clown grown wise,
Presents his forward face t' advise,
And tatter'd legislators meet
From ev'ry workshop thro' the street;   *120*
His goose the tailor finds new use in,

To patch and turn the constitution;
The blacksmith comes with sledge and grate,
To ironbind the wheels of state;
The quack forbears his patient's souse,
To purge the Council and the House,
The tinker quits his molds and doxies,
To cast assembly-men at proxies.
From dunghills deep of sable hue,
Your dirtbred patriots spring to view,   *130*
To wealth and pow'r and pension rise,
Like new-wing'd maggots chang'd to flies;
And fluttring round in proud parade,
Strut in the robe, or gay cocade.
See *Arnold quits for ways more certain,
His bankrupt perj'ries for his fortune,
Brews rum no longer in his store,
Jockey and skipper now no more;
Forsakes his warehouses and docks,
And writs of slander for the pox,   *140*
And purg'd by patriotism from shame,
Grows Gen'ral of the foremost name.

   †*Hiatus*

For in this ferment of the stream,
The dregs have work'd up to the brim,
And by the rule of topsyturvys,

* Arnold's perjuries at the time of his pretended bankruptcy, which
was the first rise of his fortune, and his curious law suit against a
brother-skipper, who had charged him with having caught the above-
mentioned disease, by his connection with a certain African princess
in the West-Indies, with its humorous issue, are matters, not I believe
so generally known, as the other circumstances of his public and
private character.
† M'Fingal having here inserted the names and characters of several
great men, whom the public have not yet fully detected, it is thought
proper to omit sundry paragraphs of his speech, in the present edition.

The skum stands swelling on the surface.
You've caus'd your pyramid t'ascend
And set it on the little end;
Like Hudibras, your empire's made,
Whose crupper had o'ertop'd his head;   *150*
You've push'd and turn'd the whole world up-
Side down and got yourselves a-top:
While all the great ones of your state,
Are crush'd beneath the pop'lar weight,
Nor can you boast this present hour,
The shadow of the form of pow'r.
For what's your Congress, or its end?
A power t' advise and recommend;
To call for troops, adjust your quotas,
And yet no soul is bound to notice;   *160*
To pawn your faith to th' utmost limit,
But cannot bind you to redeem it,
And when in want no more in them lies,
Than begging of your State-Assemblies;
Can utter oracles of dread,
Like friar Bacon's brazen head,
But should a faction e'er dispute 'em,
Has ne'er an arm to execute 'em.
As tho' you chose supreme dictators,
And put them under conservators;   *170*
You've but pursued the selfsame way,
With Shakespeare's Trinclo in the play,
"You shall be viceroys here, 'tis true,
But we'll be viceroys over you."
What wild confusion hence must ensue,
Tho' common danger yet cements you;
So some wreck'd vessel, all in shatters,
Is held up by surrounding waters,
But stranded, when the pressure ceases,
Falls by its rottenness to pieces.   *180*

And fall it must—if wars were ended,
You'll ne'er have sense enough to mend it;
But creeping on with low intrigues
Like vermin of an hundred legs,
Will find as short a life assign'd,
As all things else of reptile kind.
Your Commonwealth's a common harlot,
The property of ev'ry varlet,
Which now in taste and full employ,
All sorts admire, as all enjoy;   190
But soon a batter'd strumpet grown,
You'll curse and drum her out of town.
Such is the government you chose,
For this you bade the world be foes,
For this so mark'd for dissolution,
You scorn the British constitution,
That constitution, form'd by sages,
The wonder of all modern ages:
Which owns no failure in reality,
Except corruption and venality;   200
And only proves the adage just,
That best things spoil'd corrupt to worst.
So man supreme in mortal station,
And mighty lord of this creation,
When once his corse is dead as herring,
Becomes the most offensive carrion,
And sooner breeds the plague, 'tis found,
Than all beasts rotting 'bove the ground.
Yet for this gov'rnment, to dismay us,
You've call'd up anarchy from chaos,   210
With all the followers of her school,
Uproar and rage and wild misrule;
For whom this rout of Whigs distracted
And ravings dire of ev'ry crack'd head;
These new-cast legislative engines

Of county-musters and conventions,
Committees vile of correspondence,
And mobs, whose tricks have almost undone 's;
While reason fails to check your course,
And loyalty's kick'd out of doors,   *220*
And folly, like inviting landlord,
Hoists on your poles her royal standard.
While the king's friends in doleful dumps,
Have worn their courage to the stumps,
And leaving George in sad disaster,
Most sinfully deny their master.
What furies raged when you in sea,
In shape of Indians drown'd the tea,
When your gay sparks, fatigued to watch it,
Assumed the moggison and hatchet,   *230*
With wampom'd blankets hid their laces,
And like their sweethearts, primed their faces:
While not a redcoat dar'd oppose,
And scarce a Tory show'd his nose,
While Hutchinson for sure retreat,
Manouvred to his country seat,
And thence affrighted in the suds,
Stole off bareheaded thro' the woods!
Have you not rous'd your mobs to join,
And make Mandamus-men resign,   *240*
Call'd forth each duffil-dress'd curmudgeon,
With dirty trowsers and white bludgeon,
Forc'd all our Councils thro' the land,
To yield their necks to your command;
While paleness marks their late disgraces
Thro' all their rueful length of faces?
Have you not caused as woful work,
In loyal city of New-York,
When all the rabble well cockaded,
In triumph thro' the streets paraded;   *250*

And mobb'd the Tories, scared their spouses,
And ransack'd all the custom-houses,
Made such a tumult, bluster, jarring,
That mid the clash of tempests warring,
Smith's weathercock with veers forlorn,
Could hardly tell which way to turn;
Burnt effigies of th' higher powers,
Contriv'd in planetary hours,
As witches with clay-images,
Destroy or torture whom they please;   *260*
Till fired with rage, th' ungrateful club
Spared not your best friend, Belzebub,
O'erlook'd his favours and forgot
The rev'rence due his cloven foot,
And in the selfsame furnace frying,
Burn'd him and North and Bute and Tryon?
Did you not in as vile and shallow way,
Fright our poor Philadelphian, Galloway,
Your Congress when the daring ribald
Belied, berated and bescribbled?   *270*
What ropes and halters did you send,
Terrific emblems of his end,
Till least he'd hang in more than effigy,
Fled in a fog the trembling refugee?
Now rising in progression fatal,
Have you not ventur'd to give battle?
When treason chaced our heroes troubled,
With rusty gun and leathern doublet,
Turn'd all stonewalls and groves and bushes,
To batt'ries arm'd with blunderbusses,   *280*
And with deep wounds that fate portend,
Gaul'd many a reg'lar's latter end,
Drove them to Boston, as in jail,
Confined without mainprize or bail.
Were not these deeds enough betimes,

To heap the measure of your crimes,
But in this loyal town and dwelling,
You raise these ensigns of rebellion?
'Tis done; fair Mercy shuts her door;
And Vengeance now shall sleep no more;   290
Rise then, my friends, in terror rise,
And wipe this scandal from the skies!
You'll see their Dagon, tho' well jointed,
Will sink before the Lord's anointed,
And like old Jericho's proud wall,
Before our ram's horns prostrate fall."
    This said, our 'Squire, yet undismay'd,
Call'd forth the Constable to aid,
And bade him read in nearer station,
The riot-act and proclamation;   300
Who now advancing tow'rd the ring,
Began, "Our sov'reign Lord the King"—
When thousand clam'rous tongues he hears,
And clubs and stones assail his ears;
To fly was vain, to fight was idle,
By foes encompass'd in the middle;
In stratagem his aid he found,
And fell right craftily to ground;
Then crept to seek an hiding place,
'Twas all he could, beneath a brace;   310
Where soon the conq'ring crew espied him,
And where he lurk'd, they caught and tied him.
    At once with resolution fatal,
Both Whigs and Tories rush'd to battle;
Instead of weapons, either band
Seiz'd on such arms, as came to hand.
And as fam'd *Ovid paints th' adventures
Of wrangling Lapithae and Centaurs,

* Ovid's Metamorphoses, Book 12.

Who at their feast, by Bacchus led,
Threw bottles at each other's head,   *320*
And these arms failing in their scuffles,
Attack'd with handirons, tongs and shovels:
So clubs and billets, staves and stones
Met fierce, encount'ring ev'ry sconce,
And cover'd o'er with knobs and pains
Each void receptacle for brains;
Their clamours rend the hills around,
And earth rebellows with the sound;
And many a groan increas'd the din
From broken nose and batter'd shin.   *330*
M'Fingal rising at the word,
Drew forth his old militia sword;
Thrice cried, "King George," as erst in distress
Romancing heroes did their mistress,
And brandishing the blade in air,
Struck terror thro' th' opposing war.
The Whigs, unsafe within the wind
Of such commotion shrunk behind.
With whirling steel around address'd,
Fierce thro' their thickest throng he press'd,   *340*
(Who roll'd on either side in arch,
Like Red-sea waves in Israel's march)
And like a meteor rushing through,
Struck on their pole a vengeful blow.
Around, the Whigs, of clubs and stones
Discharg'd whole vollies in platoons,
That o'er in whistling terror fly,
But not a foe dares venture nigh.
And now perhaps with conquest crown'd,
Our 'Squire had fell'd their pole to ground;   *350*
Had not some Pow'r, a Whig at heart,
Descended down and took their part;
(Whether 'twere Pallas, Mars or Iris,

'Tis scarce worth while to make enquiries)
Who at the nick of time alarming,
Assumed the graver form of Chairman;
Address'd a Whig, in ev'ry scene
The stoutest wrestler on the green,
And pointed where the spade was found,
Late used to fix their pole in ground,   *360*
And urg'd with equal arms and might
To dare our 'Squire to single fight.*
The Whig thus arm'd, untaught to yield,
Advanc'd tremendous to the field;
Nor did M'Fingal shun the foe,
But stood to brave the desp'rate blow;
While all the party gaz'd suspended,
To see the deadly combat ended.
And Jove in equal balance weigh'd
The sword against the brandish'd spade,   *370*
He weigh'd; but lighter than a dream,
The sword flew up and kick'd the beam.
Our 'Squire on tiptoe rising fair,
Lifts high a noble stroke in air,
Which hung not, but like dreadful engines
Descended on the foe in vengeance.
But ah, in danger with dishonor
The sword perfidious fails its owner;
That sword, which oft had stood its ground
By huge trainbands encompass'd round,   *380*
Or on the bench, with blade right loyal,
Had won the day at many a trial,
Of stones and clubs had brav'd th' alarms,
Shrunk from these new Vulcanian arms.

* The learned reader will readily observe the allusions in this scene
to the single combats of Paris and Menelaus in Homer, Aeneas and
Turnus in Virgil, and Michael and Satan in Milton.

The spade so temper'd from the sledge,
Nor keen nor solid harm'd its edge,
Now met it from his arm of might
Descending with steep force to smite;
The blade snapp'd short—and from his hand
With rust embrown'd the glitt'ring sand.   390
Swift turn'd M'Fingal at the view,
And call'd for aid th' attendant crew,
In vain; the Tories all had run,
When scarce the fight was well begun;
Their setting wigs he saw decreas'd
Far in th' horizon tow'rd the west.
Amaz'd he view'd the shameful sight,
And saw no refuge but in flight:
But age unweildy check'd his pace,
Tho' fear had wing'd his flying race;   400
For not a trifling prize at stake;
No less than great M'Fingal's back.
With legs and arms he work'd his course,
Like rider that outgoes his horse,
And labour'd hard to get away, as
Old Satan *struggling on thro' chaos:
Till looking back he spied in rear
The spade-arm'd chief advanc'd too near.
Then stopp'd and seiz'd a stone that lay,
An antient land-mark near the way;   410
Nor shall we, as old Bards have done,
Affirm it weigh'd an hundred ton:
But such a stone as at a shift
A modern might suffice to lift,
Since men, to credit their enigmas,
Are dwindled down to dwarfs and pigmies,
And giants exiled with their cronies,

* In Milton.

To Brobdingnags and Patagonias.
But while our hero turn'd him round,
And stoop'd to raise it from the ground,   *420*
The deadly spade discharg'd a blow
Tremendous on his rear below:
His bent knee fail'd, and void of strength,
Stretch'd on the ground his manly length;
Like antient oak o'erturn'd he lay,
Or tow'rs to tempests fall'n a prey,
And more things else—but all men know 'em,
If slightly vers'd in Epic Poem.
At once the crew, at this sad crisis,
Fall on and bind him ere he rises,   *430*
And with loud shouts and joyful soul
Conduct him pris'ner to the pole.
   When now the Mob in lucky hour,
Had got their en'mies in their pow'r,
They first proceed by wise command
To take the constable in hand.
Then from the pole's sublimest top
They speeded to let down the rope,
At once its other end in haste bind,
And make it fast upon his waistband,   *440*
Till like the earth, as stretch'd on tenter,
He hung self-balanc'd on his center.
Then upwards all hands hoisting sail,
They swung him, like a keg of ale,
Till to the pinnacle so fair,
He rose like meteor in the air.
As *Socrates of old at first did
To aid philosophy get hoisted,
And found his thoughts flow strangely clear,

* Socrates is represented in Aristophanes's Comedy of the Clouds,
as hoisted in a basket to aid contemplation.

Swung in a basket in mid air: *450*
Our culprit thus in purer sky,
With like advantage rais'd his eye;
And looking forth in prospect wide
His Tory errors clearly spied,
And from his elevated station,
With bawling voice began addressing.
"Good gentlemen and friends and kin,
For heav'n's sake hear, if not for mine!
I here renounce the Pope, the Turks,
The King, the Devil and all their works;   *460*
And will, set me but once at ease,
Turn Whig or Christian, what you please;
And always mind your laws as justly;
Should I live long as old Methus'lah,
I'll never join with British rage,
Nor help Lord North, or Gen'ral Gage,
Nor lift my gun in future fights,
Nor take away your charter'd rights,
Nor overcome your new-rais'd levies,
Destroy your towns, nor burn your navies,   *470*
Nor cut your poles down while I've breath,
Tho' rais'd more thick than hatchel-teeth:
But leave king George and all his elves
To do their conq'ring work themselves."
    This said, they lower'd him down in state,
Spread at all points, like falling cat;
But took a vote first on the question,
That they'd accept this full confession,
And to their fellowship and favor,
Restore him on his good behaviour.   *480*
    Not so, our 'Squire submits to rule,
But stood heroic as a mule.
"You'll find it all in vain, quoth he,
To play your rebel tricks on me.

All punishments the world can render,
Serve only to provoke th' offender;
The will's confirm'd by treatment horrid,
As hides grow harder when they're curried.
No man e'er felt the halter draw,
With good opinion of the law;   *490*
Or held in method orthodox
His love of justice in the stocks;
Or fail'd to lose by sheriff's shears
At once his loyalty and ears.
Have you made Murray look less big,
Or smoak'd old Williams to a Whig?
Did our mobb'd Oliver quit his station,
Or heed his vows of resignation?
Has Rivington, in dread of stripes,
Ceas'd lying since you stole his types?   *500*
And can you think my faith will alter,
By tarring, whipping, or the halter?
I'll stand the worst; for recompence
I trust King George and Providence.
And when, our conquest gain'd, I come,
Array'd in law and terror home,
You'll rue this inauspicious morn,
And curse the day you e'er were born,
In Job's high style of imprecations,
With all his plagues, without his patience."   *510*
    Meanwhile beside the pole, the guard
A Bench of Justice had prepar'd,
Where sitting round in awful sort,
The grand Committee hold their court;
While all the crew in silent awe,
Wait from their lips the lore of law.
Few moments with deliberation,
They hold the solemn consultation,
When soon in judgment all agree,

And Clerk declares the dread decree;   520
"That 'Squire M'Fingal having grown
The vilest Tory in the town,
And now on full examination,
Convicted by his own confession,
Finding no tokens of repentance,
This Court proceed to render sentence:
That first the Mob a slip-knot single
Tie round the neck of said M'Fingal;
And in due form do tar him next,
And feather, as the law directs;   530
Then thro' the town attendant ride him,
In cart with Constable beside him,
And having held him up to shame,
Bring to the pole from whence he came."
    Forthwith the croud proceed to deck
With halter'd noose M'Fingal's neck,
While he, in peril of his soul,
Stood tied half-hanging to the pole;
Then lifting high the pond'rous jar,
Pour'd o'er his head the smoking tar: 540
With less profusion erst was spread
The Jewish oil on royal head,
That down his beard and vestments ran,
And cover'd all his outward man.
As when (so *Claudian sings) the Gods
And earth-born giants fell at odds,
The stout Enceladus in malice
Tore mountains up to throw at Pallas;
And as he held them o'er his head,
The river from their fountains fed,   550
Pour'd down his back its copious tide,
And wore its channels in his hyde:

* Claudian's Gigantomachia.

So from the high rais'd urn the torrents,
Spread down his side their various currents;
His flowing wig, as next the brim,
First met and drank the sable stream;
Adown his visage stern and grave,
Roll'd and adhered the viscid wave;
With arms depending as he stood,
Each cuff capacious holds the flood;   560
From nose and chin's remotest end,
The tarry icicles depend;
Till all o'erspread, with colors gay
He glitter'd to the western ray,
Like sleet-bound trees in wintry skies,
Or Lapland idol carv'd in ice.
And now the feather-bag display'd,
Is wav'd in triumph o'er his head,
And spreads him o'er with feathers missive,
And down upon the tar adhesive: 570
Not Maia's son, with wings for ears,
Such plumes around his visage wears;
Nor Milton's six wing'd angel gathers,
Such superfluity of feathers.
Till all compleat appears our 'Squire
Like Gorgon or Chimera dire;
Nor more could boast on *Plato's plan
To rank amid the race of man,
Or prove his claim to human nature,
As a two-legg'd, unfeather'd creature.   580
    Then on the two-wheel'd car of state,
They rais'd our grand Duumvirate.
And as at Rome a like committee,
That found an owl within their city,

* Alluding to Plato's famous definition of Man, "*Animal bipes, im-plumis.*"

With solemn rites and sad processions,
At ev'ry shrine perform'd lustrations;
And least infection should abound,
From prodigy with face so round,
All Rome attends him thro' the street,
In triumph to his country-seat;   *590*
With like devotion all the choir
Paraded round our feather'd 'Squire;
In front the martial music comes
Of horns and fiddles, fifes and drums,
With jingling sound of carriage bells,
And treble creak of rusted wheels;
Behind, the croud in lengthen'd row,
With grave procession closed the show;
And at fit period ev'ry throat
Combined in universal shout,   *600*
And hail'd great Liberty in chorus,
Or bawl'd, Confusion to the Tories.
Not louder storm the welkin braves,
From clamors of conflicting waves;
Less dire in Lybian wilds the noise
When rav'ning lions lift their voice;
Or triumphs at town-meetings made,
On passing votes to reg'late trade.
    Thus having borne them round the town,
Last at the pole they set them down,   *610*
And tow'rd the tavern take their way,
To end in mirth the festal day.
    And now the Mob dispers'd and gone,
Left 'Squire and Constable alone.
The Constable in rueful case
Lean'd sad and solemn o'er a brace,
And fast beside him, cheek by jowl,
Stuck 'Squire M'Fingal 'gainst the pole,
Glued by the tar t' his rear applied,

Like barnacle on vessel's side. 620
But tho' his body lack'd physician,
His spirit, was in worse condition.
He found his fears of whips and ropes,
By many a drachm outweigh'd his hopes.
As men in gaol without mainprize,
View ev'ry thing with other eyes,
And all goes wrong in church and state
Seen thro' perspective of the grate:
So now M'Fingal's second-sight
Beheld all things in diff'rent light; 630
His visual nerve, well purg'd with tar,
Saw all the coming scenes of war.
As his prophetic soul grew stronger,
He found he could hold in no longer;
First from the pole, as fierce he shook,
His wig from pitchy durance broke,
His mouth unglued, his feathers flutter'd,
His tarr'd skirts crack'd, and thus he utter'd.
"Ah, Mr. Constable, in vain
We strive 'gainst wind and tide and rain! 640
Behold my doom! this feather'd omen
Portends what dismal times are coming.
Now future scenes before my eyes,
And second-sighted forms arise;
I hear a voice that calls away,
And cries, the Whigs will win the day;
My beck'ning Genius gives command,
And bids us fly the fatal land;
Where changing name and constitution,
Rebellion turns to revolution, 650
While Loyalty oppress'd in tears,
Stands trembling for its neck and ears.
Go, summon all our brethren greeting,
To muster at our usual meeting.

There my prophetic voice shall warn 'em,
Of all things future that concern 'em,
And scenes disclose on which, my friend,
Their conduct and their lives depend:
There I—but first 'tis more of use,
From this vile pole to set me loose;   *660*
Then go with cautious steps and steady,
While I steer home and make all ready.

The

Vision

NOW NIGHT came down, and rose full soon
   That patroness of rogues, the Moon;
Beneath whose kind, protecting ray
Wolves, brute and human, prowl for prey.
The honest world all snored in chorus,
While owls, and ghosts and thieves and Tories,
Whom erst the mid-day sun had aw'd,
Crept from their lurking holes abroad.
On cautious hinges, slow and stiller
Wide oped the great M'Fingal's *cellar,   *10*
Where shut from prying eyes in cluster,
The Tory Pandemonium muster.
Their chiefs all sitting round descried are,

* Panditur interea domus omnipotentis Olympi,
Conciliumq; vocat Divum pater atq; hominum rex
Sideream in sedem.   *Lib. 10. Aeneid.*

On kegs of ale and seats of cyder;
When first M'Fingal dimly seen
Rose solemn from the turnep-bin.
Nor yet his †form had wholly lost
The original brightness it could boast,
Nor less appear'd than Justice Quorum,
In feather'd majesty before 'em.   *20*
Adown his tarstreak'd visage, clear
Fell glist'ning fast th' indignant tear,
And thus his voice, in mournful wise,
Pursued the prologue of his sighs.
   "Brethren and friends, the glorious band
Of loyalty in rebel land!
It was not thus you've seen me sitting
Return'd in triumph from town-meeting,
When blustring Whigs were put to stand,
And votes obey'd my guiding hand,   *30*
And new commissions pleas'd my eyes;
Blest days, but ah, no more to rise!
Alas, against my better light
And optics sure of second-sight,
My stubborn soul in error strong,
Had faith in Hutchinson too long.
See what brave trophies still we bring
From all our battles for the king;
And yet these plagues now past before us,
Are but our entring wedge of sorrows.   *40*
I see in glooms tempestuous stand
The cloud impending o'er the land;
That cloud, which still beyond their hopes
Serves all our orators with tropes,

† - - - - His form had not yet lost
All its original brightness, nor appear'd
Less than Archangel ruin'd.   *Milton.*

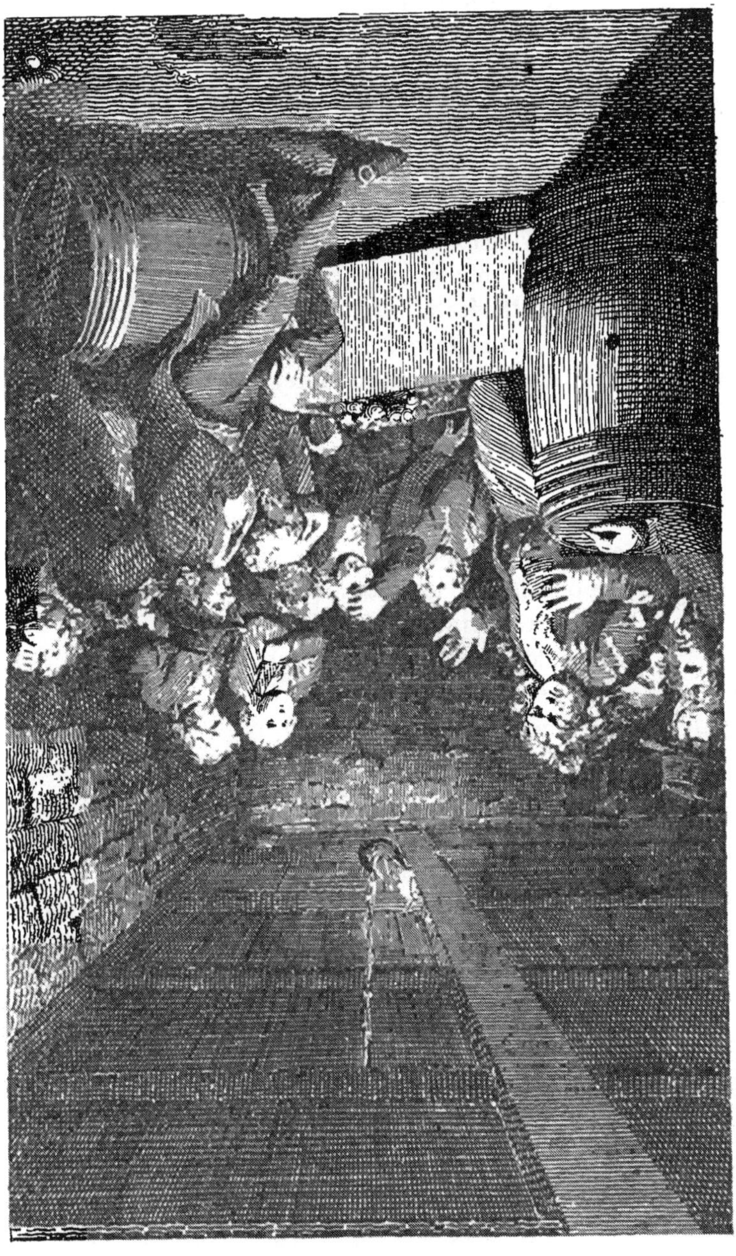

Which tho' from our own vapors fed,
Shall point its thunders on our head!
I see the Mob, beflipp'd in taverns,
Hunt us, like wolves, thro' wilds and caverns!
What dungeons rise t' alarm our fears,
What horsewhips whistle round our ears!   *50*
Tar yet in embryo in the pine
Shall run, on Tories backs to shine;
Trees rooted fair in groves of sallows
Are growing for our future gallows;
And geese unhatch'd, when pluck'd in fray,
Shall rue the feath'ring of that day.
For me, before these fatal days
I mean to fly th'accursed place,
And follow omens, which of late
Have warn'd me of impending fate;   *60*
Yet pass'd unnoticed o'er my view,
Till sad conviction proved them true;
As prophecies of best intent,
Are only heeded in th' event.
    For late in visions of the night
The gallows stood before my sight;
I saw its ladder heav'd on end;
I saw the deadly rope descend;
And in its noose that wav'ring swang,
Friend *Malcolm hung, or seem'd to hang.   *70*

* Malcolm was a Scotchman, Aid to Governor Tryon in his expedition against the Regulators in North-Carolina, where in the engage-
ment he met with the accident of the breeches here alluded to. He
was afterwards an under-officer of the customs in Boston, where becoming obnoxious, he was tarred, feathered, and half hanged by the
mob, about the year 1774. After this he was neglected and avoided
by his own party, and thinking his merits and sufferings unrewarded,
appeared equally malevolent against Whigs and Tories.
    The pretences of the Highlanders to prophecy by second-sight are
too well known to need an explanation.

How changed from him, who bold as lyon,
Stood Aid-de-Camp to Governor Tryon,
Made rebels vanish once, like witches,
And saved his life, but dropp'd his breeches.
I scarce had made a fearful bow,
And trembling ask'd him, "How d'ye do."
When lifting up his eyes so wide,
His eyes alone, his hands were tied;
With feeble voice, as spirits use,
Now almost choak'd with gripe of noose;   *80*
"Ah †fly, my friend, he cried, escape,
And keep yourself from this sad scrape;
Enough you've talk'd and writ and plann'd;
The Whigs have got the upper hand.
Dame Fortune's wheel has turn'd so short,
It plung'd us fairly in the dirt;
Could mortal arm our fears have ended,
This arm (and shook it) had defended.
But longer now 'tis vain to stay;
See ev'n the Reg'lars run away: *90*
Wait not till things grow desperater,
For hanging is no laughing matter:
This might your grandsires' fortunes tell you on
Who both were hang'd the last rebellion;
Adventure then no longer stay,
But call your friends and run away.
For lo, thro' deepest glooms of night
I come to aid thy second-sight,
Disclose the plagues that round us wait
And wake the dark decrees of fate.   *100*
Ascend this ladder whence unfurl'd
The curtain opes of t'other world,

---

† There is in this scene a general allusion to the appearance and
speech of Hector's ghost in the second book of the Eneid.

For here new worlds their scenes unfold,
Seen from this backdoor of the old.
As when Aeneas risqued his life,
Like Orpheus vent'ring for his wife,
And bore in show his mortal carcase,
Thro' realms of Erebus and Orcus,
Then in the happy fields Elysian,
Saw all his embryon sons in vision: *110*
As shown by great archangel, Michael,
Old Adam saw the world's whole sequel,
And from the mount's extended space,
The rising fortunes of his race;
So from this stage shalt thou behold,
The war its coming scenes unfold,
Rais'd by my arm to meet thine eye; /
My Adam, thou, thine Angel, I.
But first my pow'r for visions* bright,
Must cleanse from clouds thy mental sight,   *120*
Remove the dim suffusions spread,
Which bribes and sal'ries there have bred;
And from the well of Bute infuse,
Three genuine drops of Highland dews,
To purge, like euphrasy and rue,
Thine eyes, for much thou hast to view.
    Now freed from Tory darkness raise
Thy head and spy the coming days;
For lo before our second-sight,
The Continent ascends in light;   *130*
From north to south what gath'ring swarms,
Increase the pride of rebel arms!
Thro' ev'ry State our legions brave,
Speed gallant marches to the grave,
Of battling Whigs the frequent prize,

* See Milton's Paradise Lost, Book 11.

While rebel trophies stain the skies.
Behold o'er northern realms afar,
Extend the kindling flames of war!
See fam'd St. John's and Montreal,
Doom'd by Montgom'ry's arm to fall!   *140*
Where Hudson with majestic sway,
Thro' hills disparted plows his way;
Fate spreads on Bemus' Heights alarms,
And pours destruction on our arms;
There Bennington's ensanguin'd plain,
And Stony-Point, the prize of Wayne.
Behold near Del'ware's icy roar,
Where morning dawns on Trenton's shore,
While Hessians spread their Christmas feasts,
Rush rude these uninvited guests;   *150*
Nor aught avail, to Whigs a prize,
Their martial whiskers' grisly size.
On Princeton plains our heroes yield,
And spread in flight the vanquish'd field,
While fear to Mawhood's heels puts on
Wings, wide as worn by Maia's son.
Behold the Pennsylvanian shore,
Enrich'd with streams of British gore;
Where many a vet'ran chief in bed
Of honor rests his slumbring head,   *160*
And in soft vales in land of foes,
Their wearied virtue finds repose.
See plund'ring Dunmore's negro band
Fly headlong from Virginia's strand;
And far on southern hills our cousins,
The Scotch M'Donalds fall by dozens;
Or where King's Mountain lifts its head,
Our ruin'd bands in triumph led!
Behold o'er Tarlton's blustring train,
The Rebels stretch the captive chain!   *170*

Afar near Eutaw's fatal springs
Descending Vict'ry spreads her wings!
Thro' all the land in various chace,
We hunt the rainbow of success;
In vain! their Chief superior still
Eludes our force with Fabian skill,
Or swift descending by surprize,
Like Prussia's eagle sweeps the prize."
   I look'd, nor yet, opprest with fears,
Gave credit to my eyes or ears,   *180*
But held the views an empty dream,
On Berkly's immaterial scheme;
And pondring sad with troubled breast
At length my rising doubts express'd.
"Ah whither, thus by rebels smitten,
Is fled th' omnipotence of Britain,
Or fail'd its usual guard to keep,
Gone truanting or fall'n asleep;
As Baal his prophets left confounded,
And bawling vot'ries gash'd and wounded?   *190*
Did not, retir'd to bow'rs Elysian,
Great Mars leave with her his commission,
And Neptune erst in treaty free,
Give up dominion o'er the sea?
Else where's the faith of famed orations,
Address, debate and proclamations,
Or courtly sermon, laureat ode,
And ballads on the watry God;
With whose high strains great George enriches
His eloquence of gracious speeches?   *200*
Not faithful to our Highland eyes,
These deadly forms of vision rise;
But sure some Whig-inspiring sprite
Now palms delusion on our sight.
I'd scarcely trust a tale so vain,

Should revelation prompt the strain,
Or Ossian's ghost the scenes rehearse,
In all the melody of *Erse."
   "Too long, quoth Malcolm, with confusion
You've dwelt already in delusion,   *210*
As Sceptics, of all fools the chief,
Hold faith in creeds of unbelief.
I come to draw thy veil aside
Of error, prejudice and pride.
Fools love deception, but the wise
Prefer sad truths to pleasing lies.
For know those hopes can ne'er succeed
That trust on Britain's breaking reed.
For weak'ning long from bad to worse
By fatal atrophy of purse,   *220*
She feels at length with trembling heart,
Her foes have found her mortal part.
As famed Achilles, dipt by Thetis
In Styx, as sung in antient ditties,
Grew all caseharden'd o'er like steel,
Invulnerable, save his heel,
And laugh'd at swords and spears, as squibs,
And all diseases, but the kibes;
Yet met at last his fatal wound,
By Paris' arrow nail'd to ground: *230*
So Britain's boasted strength deserts,
In these her empire's utmost skirts,
Remov'd beyond her fierce impressions,
And atmosphere of omnipresence;
Nor to these shores remoter ends,
Her dwarf omnipotence extends:
Whence in this turn of things so strange,

* Erse, the antient Scottish language, in which Ossian wrote his
poems.

'Tis time our principles to change.
For vain that boasted faith, which gathers
No perquisite, but tar and feathers,   *240*
No pay, but Whig's insulting malice,
And no promotion, but the gallows.
I've long enough stood firm and steady,
Half hang'd for loyalty already:
And could I save my neck and pelf
I'd turn a flaming Whig myself,
And quit this cause and course and calling,
Like rats that fly from house that's falling.
But since, obnoxious here to fate,
This saving wisdom comes too late,   *250*
Our noblest hopes already crost,
Our sal'ries gone, our titles lost,
Doom'd to worse suff'rings from the mob,
Than Satan's surg'ries used on Job;
What more remains but now with sleight,
What's left of us to save by flight?
    Now raise thine eyes for visions true
Again ascending wait thy view."
I look'd and clad in early light,
The spires of Boston rose to sight;   *260*
The morn o'er eastern hills afar,
Illum'd the varying scenes of war.
Great Howe had long since in the lap
Of Loring taken out his nap,
And with the sun's ascending ray,
The cuckold came to take his pay.
When all th' encircling hills around,
With instantaneous breastworks crown'd,
With pointed thunders met his sight,
By magic rear'd the former night.   *270*
Each summit, far as eye commands,
Shone peopled with rebellious bands.

Aloft their tow'ring heroes rise,
As Titans erst assail'd the skies,
Leagued with superior force to prove,
The scepter'd hand of British Jove.
Mounds piled on hills ascended fair
With batt'ries placed in middle air,
That rais'd like angry clouds on high
Seem'd like th' artill'ry of the sky,   280
And hurl'd their fiery bolts amain,
In thunder on the trembling plain.
I saw along the prostrate strand,
Our baffled Gen'rals quit the land,
And swift as frighted mermaids flee,
T' our boasted element, the sea!
Resign that long contested shore,
Again the prize of rebel-power,
And tow'rd their town of refuge fly,
Like convict Jews condemn'd to die.   290
   Then tow'rd the north, I turn'd my eyes,
Where Saratoga's heights arise,
And saw our chosen vet'ran band,
Descend in terror o'er the land;
T' oppose this fury of alarms,
Saw all New-England wake to arms,
And ev'ry Yanky full of mettle,
Swarm forth, like bees at sound of kettle.
Not Rome, when Tarquin raped Lucretia,
Saw wilder mustring of militia.   300
Thro' all the woods and plains of fight,
What mortal battles fill'd my sight,
While British corses strew'd the shore,
And Hudson ting'd his streams with gore!
What tongue can tell the dismal day,
Or paint the party-color'd fray;
When yeomen left their fields afar,

To plow the crimson plains of war;
When zeal to swords transformed their shares,
And turn'd their pruning-hooks to spears,   *310*
Chang'd tailor's geese to guns and ball,
And stretch'd to pikes the cobler's awl;
While hunters fierce like mighty Nimrod,
Made on our troops a daring inroad;
And levelling squint on barrel round,
Brought our beau-officers to ground;
While rifle-frocks sent Gen'rals cap'ring,
And redcoats shrunk from leathern apron,
And epaulette and gorget run
From whinyard brown and rusty gun: *320*
While sunburnt wigs in high command,
Rush furious on our frighted band,
And antient beards and hoary hair,
Like meteors stream in troubled air.
With locks unshorn not Samson more
Made useless all the show of war,
Nor fought with asses jaw for rarity,
With more success or singularity.
I saw our vet'ran thousands yield
And pile their muskets on the field,   *330*
And peasant guards in rueful plight
March off our captured bands from fight;
While ev'ry rebel-fife in play,
To Yanky-doodle tun'd its lay,
And like the music of the spheres,
Mellifluous sooth'd their vanquish'd ears.
      "Alas, said I, what baleful star,
Sheds fatal influence on the war,
And who that chosen Chief of fame,
That heads this grand parade of shame?"   *340*
      "There see how fate, great Malcolm cried,
Strikes with its bolts the tow'rs of pride.

Behold that martial Macaroni,
Compound of Phoebus and Bellona,
With warlike sword and singsong lay,
Equipp'd alike for feast or fray,
Where equal wit and valour join;
This, this is he, the famed Burgoyne:
Who pawn'd his honor and commission,
To coax the Patriots to submission,   *350*
By songs and balls secure obedience,
And dance the ladies to allegiance.
Oft his camp muses he'll parade,
At Boston in the grand blockade,
And well invoked with punch of arrack,
Hold converse sweet in tent or barrack,
Inspired in more heroic fashion,
Both by his theme and situation;
While farce and proclamation grand,
Rise fair beneath his plastic hand.   *360*
For genius swells more strong and clear
When close confin'd, like bottled beer:
So Prior's wit gain'd greater pow'r,
By inspiration of the tow'r;
And Raleigh fast in prison hurl'd
Wrote all the hist'ry of the world:
So Wilkes grew, while in gaol he lay,
More patriotic ev'ry day,
But found his zeal, when not confin'd,
Soon sink below the freezing point,   *370*
And public spirit once so fair,
Evaporate in open air.
But thou, great favorite of Venus,
By no such luck shalt cramp thy genius;
Thy friendly stars till wars shall cease,
Shall ward th' illfortune of release,
And hold thee fast in bonds not feeble,

In good condition still to scribble.
Such merit fate shall shield from firing,
Bomb, carcase, langridge and cold iron,   *380*
Nor trusts thy doubly laurell'd head,
To rude assaults of flying lead.
Hence in this Saratogue retreat,
For pure good fortune thou'lt be beat;
Nor taken oft, releas'd or rescued,
Pass for small change, like simple Prescott;
But captured there, as fates befall,
Shalt stand thy hand for't, once for all.
Then raise thy daring thoughts sublime,
And dip thy conq'ring pen in rhyme,   *390*
And changing war for puns and jokes,
Write new Blockades and Maids of Oaks*."
    This said, he turn'd, and saw the tale,
Had dyed my trembling cheeks with pale;
Then pitying in a milder vein
Pursued the visionary strain.
    "Too much perhaps hath pain'd your views
Of vic'tries gain'd by rebel crews;
Now see the deeds not small or scanty,
Of British Valor and Humanity;   *400*
And learn from this auspicious sight,
How England's sons and friends can fight,
In what dread scenes their courage grows,
And how they conquer all their foes."
    I look'd and saw in wintry skies
Our spacious prison-walls arise,
Where Britons all their captives taming,
Plied them with scourging, cold and famine;

* The Maid of the Oaks and the Blockade of Boston, are farces—
the first acknowledged by General Burgoyne, the other generally
ascribed to him.

Reduced to life's concluding stages,
By noxious food and plagues contagious.   410
Aloft the mighty Loring stood,
And thrived, like *Vampyre, on their blood,
And counting all his gains arising,
Dealt daily rations out of poison.
Amid the dead that croud the scene,
The moving skeletons were seen.
At hand our troops in vaunting strains,
Insulted all their wants and pains,
And turn'd on all the dying tribe,
The bitter taunt and scornful gibe: 420
And British officers of might,
Triumphant at the joyful sight,
O'er foes disarm'd with courage daring,
Exhausted all their tropes of swearing.
Around all stain'd with rebel blood,
Like Milton's lazar house it stood,
Where grim Despair attended nurse,
And Death was Gov'rnor of the house.
Amaz'd I cried, "Is this the way,
That British Valour wins the day?"   430
More had I said, in strains unwelcome,
Till interrupted thus by Malcolm:
"Blame not, quoth he, but learn the reason
Of this new mode of conq'ring treason.
'Tis but a wise, politic plan,
To root out all the rebel-clan;
(For surely treason ne'er can thrive,
Where not a soul is left alive:)
A scheme, all other chiefs to surpass,

* The notion of Vampyres is a superstition, that has greatly pre-
vailed in many parts of Europe. They pretend it is a dead body,
which rises out of its grave in the night, and sucks the blood of the
living.

And to do th' effectual work to purpose.   *440*
For war itself is nothing further,
But th' art and mystery of murther,
And who most methods has essay'd,
Is the best Gen'ral of the trade,
And stands Death's Plenipotentiary,
To conquer, poison, starve and bury.
This Howe well knew, and thus began,
(Despising Carlton's coaxing plan,
Who kept his pris'ners well and merry,
And dealt them food like Commissary,   *450*
And by paroles and ransoms vain,
Dismisss'd them all to fight again:)
Whence his first captives with great spirit,
He tied up for his troops to fire* at,
And hoped they'd learn on foes thus taken,
To aim at rebels without shaking.
Then wise in stratagem he plann'd
The sure destruction of the land,
Turn'd famine, sickness and despair,
To useful enginry of war,   *460*
Instead of cannon, musket, mortar,
Used pestilence and death and torture,
Sent forth the small pox and the greater,
To thin the land of ev'ry traitor,
And order'd out with like endeavour,
Detachments of the prison-fever;
Spread desolation o'er their head,
And plagues in Providence's stead,
Perform'd with equal skill and beauty,
Th' avenging angel's tour of duty,   *470*
Brought all the elements to join,

* This was done openly and without censure by the troops under
Howe's command in many instances, on his first conquest of Long-
Island.

And stars t' assist the great design,
As once in league with Kishon's brook,
Famed Israel's foes they fought and took.
Then proud to raise a glorious name,
And em'lous of his country's fame,
He bade these prison-walls arise,
Like temple tow'ring to the skies,
Where British Clemency renown'd,
Might fix her seat on sacred ground;   *480*
(That Virtue, as each herald saith,
Of whole blood kin to Punic Faith)
Where all her Godlike pow'rs unveiling,
She finds a grateful shrine to dwell in.
Then at this altar for her honor,
Chose this Highpriest to wait upon her,
Who with just rites, in antient guises,
Presents these human sacrifices;
Great Loring, famed above laymen,
A proper Priest for Lybian Ammon,   *490*
Who, while Howe's gift his brows adorns,
Had match'd that deity in horns.
Here ev'ry day her vot'ries tell
She more devours than th' idol Bel;
And thirsts more rav'nously for gore,
Than any worshipp'd Pow'r before.
That antient Heathen Godhead, Moloch,
Oft stay'd his stomach with a bullock,
Or if his morning rage you'd check first,
One child sufficed him for a breakfast.   *500*
But British Clemency with zeal
Devours her hundreds at a meal,
Right well by Nat'ralists defined,
A Being of carniv'rous kind.
So erst *Gargantua pleas'd his palate,

* See Rabelais's history of the giant Gargantua.

And eat his pilgrims up for sallad.
Not blest with maw less ceremonious,
The wide-mouth'd whale that swallow'd Jonas,
Like earthquake gapes, to death devote,
That open sepulchre, her throat;   *510*
The grave, or barren womb you'd stuff,
And sooner bring to cry, enough;
Or fatten up to fair condition,
The leanflesh'd kine of Pharaoh's vision.
   Behold her temple where it stands
Erect by famed Britannic hands;
'Tis the blackhole of Indian structure,
New-built with English architecture,
On plan, 'tis said, contrived and wrote,
By Clive, before he cut his throat;   *520*
Who ere he took himself in hand,
Was her Highpriest in Nabob-land:
And when with conq'ring glory crown'd,
He'd well enslav'd the nation round,
With pitying heart the gen'rous chief,
(Since slav'ry's worse than loss of life)
Bade desolation circle far,
And famine end the work of war;
Thus loosed their chains and for their merits,
Dismiss'd them free to worlds of spirits: *530*
Whence they with gratitude and praise,
Return'd* to attend his latter days,
And hov'ring round his restless bed,
Spread nightly visions o'er his head.
   "Now turn, he cried, to nobler sights,
And mark the prowess of our fights:

---

* Clive in the latter years of his life conceived himself perpetually haunted by the ghosts of those, who were the victims of his British humanity in the East-Indies.

Behold like whelps of British Lyon,
The warriors, Clinton, Vaughan and Tryon,
March forth with patriotic joy,
To ravish, plunder, burn, destroy.   *540*
Great Gen'rals foremost in the nation,
The journeymen of Desolation!
Like Samson's foxes each assails,
Let loose with firebrands in their tails,
And spreads destruction more forlorn,
Than they did in Philistine corn.
And see in flames their triumphs rise,
Illuming all the nether skies,
And streaming, like a new Aurora,
The western hemisphere with glory!   *550*
What towns in ashes laid confess
These heroes' prowess and success!
What blacken'd walls, or burning fane,
For trophies spread the ruin'd plain!
What females caught in evil hour,
By force submit to British power,
Or plunder'd Negroes in disaster
Confess king George their lord and master!
What crimson corses strew their way
Till smoking carnage dims the day!   *560*
Along the shore for sure reduction
They wield their besom of destruction.
Great Homer likens, in his Ilias,
To dogstar bright the fierce Achilles;
But ne'er beheld in red procession,
Three dogstars rise in constellation;
Or saw in glooms of ev'ning misty,
Such signs of fiery triplicity,
Which far beyond the comet's tail,
Portend destruction where they sail.   *570*
Oh had Great-Britain's godlike shore,

Produced but ten such heroes more,
They'd spared the pains and held the station,
Of this world's final conflagration,
Which when its time comes, at a stand,
Would find its work all done t' its hand!
    Yet tho' gay hopes our eyes may bless;
Indignant fate forbids success;
Like morning dreams our conquest flies,
Dispers'd before the dawn arise."   *580*
    Here Malcolm paus'd; when pond'ring long,
Grief thus gave utt'rance to my tongue.
"Where shrink in fear our friends dismay'd,
And all the Tories' promis'd aid,
Can none amid these fierce alarms
Assist the pow'r of royal arms?"
"In vain, he cried, our king depends,
On promis'd aid of Tory-friends.
When our own efforts want success,
Friends ever fail as fears increase.   *590*
As leaves in blooming verdure wove,
In warmth of summer cloath the grove,
But when autumnal frosts arise,
Leave bare their trunks to wintry skies;
So while your pow'r can aid their ends,
You ne'er can need ten thousand friends,
But once in want by foes dismay'd,
May advertise them stol'n or stray'd.
Thus ere Great-Britain's strength grew slack,
She gain'd that aid, she did not lack,   *600*
But now in dread, imploring pity,
All hear unmov'd her dol'rous ditty;
Allegiance wand'ring turns astray,
And Faith grows dim for lack of pay.
In vain she tries by new inventions,
Fear, falshood, flatt'ry, threats and pensions,

Or sends Commiss'ners with credentials
Of promises and penitentials.
As for his fare o'er Styx of old,
The Trojan stole the bough of gold,   *610*
And least grim Cerberus should make head,
Stuff'd both his fobs with *gingerbread;
Behold at Britain's utmost shifts,
Comes Johnstone loaded with like gifts,
To venture thro' the Whiggish tribe,
To cuddle, wheedle, coax and bribe,
Enter their lands and on his journey,
Possession take, as King's Attorney,
Buy all the vassals to protect him,
And bribe the tenants not t' eject him;   *620*
And call to aid his desp'rate mission,
His petticoated politician,
While Venus join'd t' assist the farce,
Strolls forth Embassador for Mars.
In vain he strives, for while he lingers,
These mastiffs bite his off'ring fingers;
Nor buys for George and realms infernal,
One spaniel, but the mongrel Arnold.
    " 'Twere vain to paint in vision'd show,
The mighty nothings done by Howe;   *630*
What towns he takes in mortal fray,
As stations, whence to run away;
What conquests gain'd in battles warm,
To us no aid, to them no harm;
For still the event alike is fatal,
What'er success attend the battle,
If he gain victory, or lose it,
Who ne'er had skill enough to use it;
And better 'twere at their expence,

* ——Medicatam frugibus offam.
          Aeneid. lib. 6, lin. 410.

T' have drubb'd him into common sense,   *640*
And wak'd by bastings on his rear,
Th' activity, tho' but of fear.
By slow advance his arms prevail,
Like emblematic march of snail;
That be Millennium nigh or far,
'Twould long before him end the war.
From York to Philadelphian ground,
He sweeps the mighty flourish round,
Wheel'd circ'lar by excentric stars,
Like racing boys at prison-bars,   *650*
Who take the adverse crew in whole,
By running round the opp'site goal;
Works wide the traverse of his course,
Like ship in storms' opposing force,
Like millhorse circling in his race,
Advances not a single pace,
And leaves no trophies of reduction,
Save that of cankerworms, destruction.
Thus having long both countries curst,
He quits them, as he found them first,   *660*
Steers home disgraced, of little worth,
To join Burgoyne and rail at North.
    Now raise thine eyes, and view with pleasure,
The triumphs of his famed successor."
I look'd, and now by magic lore,
Faint rose to view the Jersey shore;
But dimly seen, in glooms array'd,
For Night had pour'd her sable shade,
And ev'ry star, with glimm'rings pale,
Was muffled deep in ev'ning veil: *670*
Scarce visible in dusky night,
Advancing redcoats rose to sight;
The lengthen'd train in gleaming rows
Stole silent from their slumb'ring foes,

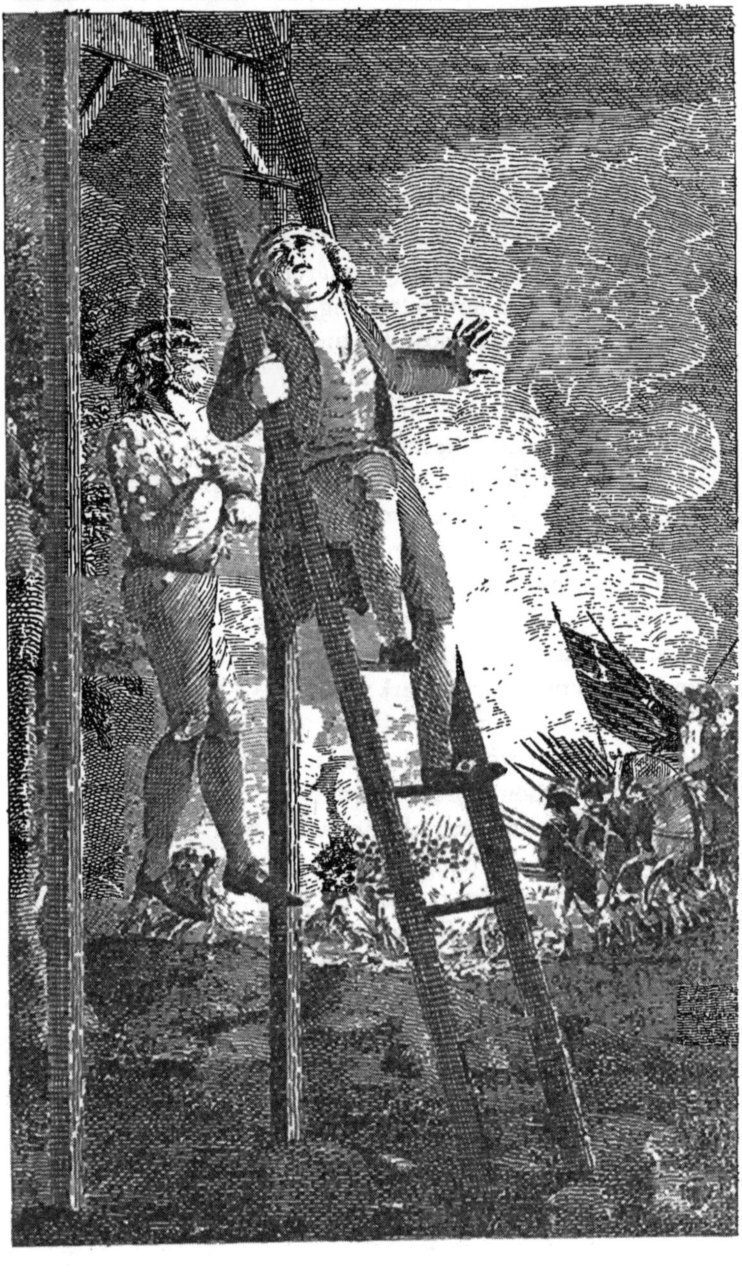

Slow moved the baggage and the train,
Like snail crept noiseless o'er the plain;
No trembling soldier dared to speak,
And not a wheel presum'd to creak.
My looks my new surprise confess'd,
Till by great Malcolm thus address'd: 680
"Spend not thy wits in vain researches;
'Tis one of Clinton's moonlight marches.
From Philadelphia now retreating,
To save his anxious troops a beating,
With hasty stride he flies in vain,
His rear attack'd on Monmouth plain:
With various chance the mortal fray
Is lengthen'd to the close of day,
When his tired bands o'ermatch'd in fight,
Are rescued by descending night;   690
He forms his camp with vain parade,
Till ev'ning spreads the world with shade,
Then still, like some endanger'd spark,
Steals off on tiptoe in the dark;
Yet writes his king in boasting tone,
How grand he march'd by light of moon.
I see him; but thou canst not; proud
He leads in front the trembling croud,
And wisely knows, if danger's near,
'Twill fall the heaviest on his rear.   700
Go on, great Gen'ral, nor regard
The scoffs of ev'ry scribling Bard,
Who sing how Gods that fatal night
Aided by miracles your flight,
As once they used, in Homer's day,
To help weak heroes run away;
Tell how the hours at awful trial,
Went back, as erst on Ahaz' dial,
While British Joshua stay'd the moon,

On Monmouth plains for Ajalon: *710*
Heed not their sneers and gibes so arch,
Because she set before your march.
A small mistake, your meaning right,
You take her influence for her light;
Her influence, which shall be your guide,
And o'er your Gen'ralship preside.
Hence still shall teem your empty skull,
With vict'ries when the moon's at full,
Which by transition yet more strange,
Wane to defeats before the change;   *720*
Hence all your movements, all your notions
Shall steer by like excentric motions,
Eclips'd in many a fatal crisis,
And dimm'd when Washington arises.
And see how Fate, herself turn'd traitor,
Inverts the antient course of nature,
And changes manners, tempers, climes,
To suit the genius of the times.
See Bourbon forms his gen'rous plan,
First guardian of the rights of man,   *730*
And prompt in firm alliance joins,
To aid the Rebels proud designs.
Behold from realms of eastern day,
His sails innum'rous shape their way,
In warlike line the billows sweep,
And roll the thunders of the deep.
See low in equinoctial skies,
The Western Islands fall their prize.
See British flags o'ermatch'd in might,
Put all their faith in instant flight,   *740*
Or broken squadrons from th' affray,
Drag slow their wounded hulks away.
Behold his chiefs in daring setts,
D'Estaings, De Grasses and Fayettes,

Spread thro' our camps their dread alarms,
And swell the fears of rebel-arms.
Yet ere our empire sink in night,
One gleam of hope shall strike the sight;
As lamps that fail of oil and fire,
Collect one glimmring to expire.   *750*
And lo where southern shores extend,
Behold our union'd hosts descend,
Where Charlestown views with varying beams,
Her turrets gild th' encircling streams.
There by superior might compell'd,
Behold their gallant Lincoln yield,
Nor aught the wreaths avail him now,
Pluck'd from Burgoyne's imperious brow.
See furious from the vanquish'd strand,
Cornwallis leads his might band!   *760*
The southern realms and Georgian shore
Submit and own the victor's pow'r,
Lo sunk before his wasting way,
The Carolinas fall his prey!
In vain embattled hosts of foes
Essay in warring strife t' oppose.
See shrinking from his conq'ring eye,
The rebel legions fall or fly;
And with'ring in these torrid skies,
The northern laurel fades and dies.   *770*
With rapid force he leads his band
To fair Virginia's fated strand,
Triumphant eyes the travell'd zone,
And boasts the southern realms his own.
Nor yet this hero's glories bright
Blaze only in the fields of fight,
Not Howe's humanity more deserving,
In gifts of hanging and of starving;
Not Arnold plunders more tobacco,

Or steals more Negroes for Jamaica;   *780*
Scarce Rodney's self among th' Eustatians,
Insults so well the laws of nations;
Ev'n Tryon's fame grows dim, and mourning,
He yields the laurel crown of burning.
I see with rapture and surprize,
New triumphs sparkling in thine eyes.
But view where now renew'd in might,
Again the rebels dare the fight."
   I look'd and far in southern skies,
Saw Greene, their second hope, arise,   *790*
And with his small but gallant band,
Invade the Carolinian land.
As winds in stormy circles whirl'd
Rush billowing o'er the darken'd world,
And where their wasting fury roves,
Successive sweep th' astonish'd groves.
Thus where he pours the rapid fight,
Our boasted conquests sink in night,
And wide o'er all th' extended field,
Our forts resign, our armies yield,   *800*
Till now regain'd the vanquish'd land,
He lifts his standard on the strand.
   Again to fair Virginia's coast,
I turn'd and view'd the British host,
Where Chesapeak's wide waters lave
Her shores and join th' Atlantic wave.
There fam'd Cornwallis tow'ring rose,
And scorn'd secure his distant foes;
His bands the haughty rampart raise,
And bid th' imperial standard blaze.   *810*
When lo, where ocean's bounds extend,
I saw the Gallic sails ascend,
With fav'ring breezes stem their way,
And croud with ships the spacious bay.

Lo Washington from northern shores,
O'er many a region, wheels his force,
And Rochambeau, with legions bright,
Descends in terrors to the fight.
Not swifter cleaves his rapid way,
The eagle cow'ring o'er his prey,   *820*
Or knights in fam'd romance that fly
On fairy 'pinions thro' the sky.
Amaz'd the Briton's startled pride,
Sees ruin wake on ev'ry side;
And all his troops to fate consign'd,
By instantaneous stroke Burgoyn'd.
Not Cadmus view'd with more surprize,
From earth embattled armies rise,
When by superior pow'r impell'd,
He sow'd with dragon's teeth the field.   *830*
Here Gallic troops in terror stand,
There rush in arms the Rebel band;
Nor hope remains from mortal fight,
Or that last British refuge, flight.
I saw with looks downcast and grave,
The Chief emerging from his *cave,
(Where chaced like hare in mighty round,
His hunters earth'd him first in ground)
And doom'd by fate to rebel sway,
Yield all his captur'd hosts a prey.   *840*
    There while I view'd the vanquish'd town,
Thus with a sigh my friend went on:
"Beholdst thou not that band forlorn,
Like slaves in Roman triumphs borne;
Their faces length'ning with their fears,
And cheeks distain'd with streams of tears,

---

* Alluding to the well known fact of Cornwallis's taking up his resi-
dence in a cave, during the siege of York-Town.

Like *dramatis personae* sage,
Equipt to act on Tyburn's stage.
Lo these are they, who lur'd by follies,
Left all and follow'd great Cornwallis;   *850*
True to their King, with firm devotion,
For conscience sake and hop'd promotion,
Expectant of the promis'd glories,
And new Millennial state of Tories.
Alas, in vain, all doubts forgetting,
They tried th' omnipotence of Britain;
But found her arm, once strong and brave,
So shorten'd now she cannot save.
Not more aghast departed souls,
Who risk'd their fate on Popish bulls,   *860*
And find St. Peter at the wicket
Refuse to countersign their ticket,
When driv'n to purgatory back,
With all their pardons in their pack:
Than Tories must'ring at their stations
On faith of royal proclamations.
As Pagan Chiefs at ev'ry crisis,
Confirm'd their leagues by sacrifices,
And herds of beasts to all their deities,
Oblations fell at close of treaties: *870*
Cornwallis thus in antient fashion,
Concludes his league of cap'tulation,
And victims due to Rebel-glories,
Gives this sin-off'ring up of Tories.
See where reliev'd from sad embargo,
Steer off consign'd a recreant cargo,
Like old scapegoats to roam in pain,
Mark'd like their great forerunner, Cain.
The rest, now doom'd by British leagues,
To justice of resentful Whigs,   *880*
Hold worthless lives on tenure ill,

Of tenancy at Rebel-will,
While hov'ring o'er their forfeit persons,
The gallows waits his sure reversions.
   Thou too, M'Fingal, ere that day,
Shalt taste the terrors of th' affray.
See o'er thee hangs in angry skies,
Where Whiggish constellations rise,
And while plebeian signs ascend,
Their mob-inspiring aspects bend;   890
That baleful Star, whose *horrid hair
Shakes forth the plagues of down and tar!
I see the pole, that rears on high
Its flag terrific thro' the sky;
The Mob beneath prepar'd t' attack,
And tar predestin'd for thy back!
Ah quit, my friend, this dang'rous home,
Nor wait the darker scenes to come;
For know that Fate's auspicious door,
Once shut to flight is oped no more,   900
Nor wears its hinge by various stations,
Like Mercy's door in proclamations.
   But lest thou pause, or doubt to fly,
To stranger visions turn thine eye:
Each cloud that dimm'd thy mental ray,
And all the mortal mists decay;
See more than human Pow'rs befriend,
And lo their hostile forms ascend!
See tow'ring o'er th' extended strand,
The Genius of the western land,   910
In vengeance arm'd, his sword assumes,
And stands, like Tories, drest in plumes.
See o'er yon Council seat with pride,

* —— From his horrid hair
Shakes pestilence and war.   Milton.

How Freedom spreads her banners wide!
There Patriotism with torch address'd,
To fire with zeal each daring breast!
While all the Virtues in their band,
Escape from yon unfriendly land,
Desert their antient British station,
Possest with rage of emigration.   *920*
Honor, his business at a stand,
For fear of starving quits their land;
And Justice, long disgraced at Court, had
By Mansfield's sentence been transported.
Vict'ry and Fame attend their way,
Tho' Britain wish their longer stay,
Care not what George or North would be at,
Nor heed their writs of *ne exeat;*
But fired with love of colonizing,
Quit the fall'n empire for the rising."   *930*
    I look'd and saw with horror smitten,
These hostile pow'rs averse to Britain.
When lo, an awful spectre rose,
With languid paleness on his brows;
Wan dropsies swell'd his form beneath,
And iced his bloated cheeks with death;
His tatter'd robes exposed him bare,
To ev'ry blast of ruder air;
On two weak crutches propt he stood,
That bent at ev'ry step he trod,   *940*
Gilt titles graced their sides so slender,
One, "Regulation," t'other, "Tender;"
His breastplate grav'd with various dates,
"The faith of all th' United States:"
Before him went his fun'ral pall,
His grave stood dug to wait his fall.
I started, and aghast I cried,
"What means this spectre at their side?

What danger from a Pow'r so vain,
And why he joins that splendid train?"   *950*
"Alas, great Malcolm cried, experience
Might teach you not to trust appearance.
Here stands, as drest by fierce Bellona,
The ghost of Continental Money,
Of dame Necessity descended,
With whom Credulity engender'd.
Tho' born with constitution frail,
And feeble strength that soon must fail;
Yet strangely vers'd in magic lore,
And gifted with transforming pow'r.   *960*
His skill the wealth Peruvian joins
With diamonds of Brazilian mines.
As erst Jove fell by subtle wiles
On Danae's apron thro' the tiles,
In show'rs of gold; his potent hand
Shall shed like show'rs thro' all the land.
Less great the magic art was reckon'd,
Of tallies cast by Charles the second,
Or Law's famed Mississipi schemes,
Or all the wealth of Southsea dreams.   *970*
For he of all the world alone
Owns the longsought Philos'pher's stone,
Restores the fab'lous times to view,
And proves the tale of Midas true.
O'er heaps of rags, he waves his wand,
All turn to gold at his command,
Provide for present wants and future,
Raise armies, victual, clothe, accoutre,
Adjourn our conquests by essoign,
Check Howe's advance and take Burgoyne,   *980*
Then makes all days of payment vain,
And turns all back to rags again.
In vain great Howe shall play his part,

To ape and counterfeit his art;
In vain shall Clinton, more belated,
A conj'rer turn to imitate it;
With like ill luck and pow'r as narrow,
They'll fare, like for'cers of old Pharaoh,
Who tho' the art they understood
Of turning rivers into blood,   990
And caus'd their frogs and snakes t' exist,
That with some merit croak'd and hiss'd,
Yet ne'er by ev'ry quaint device,
Could frame the true Mosaic lice.
He for the Whigs his arts shall try,
Their first, and long their sole ally;
A patriot firm, while breath he draws,
He'll perish in his country's cause;
And when his magic labours cease,
Lie buried in eternal peace.   1000
   Now view the scenes in future hours,
That wait the famed European Pow'rs.
See where yon chalky cliffs arise,
The hills of Britain strike your eyes:
Its small extension long supplied,
By vast immensity of pride;
So small, that had it found a station
In this new world at first creation,
Or were by Justice doom'd to suffer,
And for its crimes transported over,   1010
We'd find full room for't in lake Eri, or
The larger waterpond, Superior,
Where North on margin taking stand,
Would not be able to spy land.
No more, elate with pow'r, at ease
She deals her insults round the seas;
See dwindling from her height amain,
What piles of ruin spread the plain;

With mould'ring hulks her ports are fill'd,
And brambles clothe the cultur'd field!   1020
See on her cliffs her Genius lies,
His handkerchief at both his eyes,
With many a deepdrawn sigh and groan,
To mourn her ruin and his own!
While joyous Holland, France and Spain,
With conq'ring navies rule the main,
And Russian banners wide unfurl'd,
Spread commerce round the eastern world.
And see (sight hateful and tormenting)
Th' Amer'can empire proud and vaunting,   1030
From anarchy shall change her crasis,
And fix her pow'r on firmer basis;
To glory, wealth and fame ascend,
Her commerce rise, her realms extend;
Where now the panther guards his den,
Her desart forests swarm with men,
Her cities, tow'rs and columns rise,
And dazzling temples meet the skies;
Her pines descending to the main,
In triumph spread the watry plain,   1040
Ride inland lakes with fav'ring gales,
And croud her ports with whit'ning sails;
Till to the skirts of western day,
The peopled regions own her sway."
    Thus far M'Fingal told his tale,
When thundring shouts his ears assail,
And strait a Tory that stood centry,
Aghast rush'd headlong down the entry,
And with wild outcry, like magician,
Dispers'd the residue of vision: 1050
For now the Whigs intell'gence found
Of Tories mustring under ground,
And with rude bangs and loud uproar,

'Gain thunder furious at the door.
The lights put out, each Tory calls
To cover him, on cellar walls,
Creeps in each box, or bin, or tub,
To hide his head from wrath of mob,
Or lurks, where cabbages in row
Adorn'd the side with verdant show.   *1060*
M'Fingal deem'd it vain to stay,
And risk his bones in second fray;
But chose a grand retreat from foes,
In lit'ral sense, beneath their nose.
The window then, which none else knew,
He softly open'd and crept thro'
And crawling slow in deadly fear,
By movements wise made good his rear.
Then scorning all the fame of martyr,
For Boston took his swift departure;   *1070*
Nor dar'd look back on fatal spot,
More than the family of Lot.
Not North in more distress'd condition,
Outvoted first by opposition:
Nor good king George when that dire phantom
Of Independence comes to haunt him,
Which hov'ring round by night and day,
Not all his conj'rers yet can lay.
His friends, assembled for his sake,
He wisely left in pawn at stake,   *1080*
Of tarring, feath'ring, kicks and drubs
Of furious, disappointed mobs,
And with their forfeit hides to pay
For him, their leader, crept away.
So when wise Noah summon'd greeting
All animals to gen'ral meeting;
From ev'ry side the members sent
All kinds of beasts to represent;

Each from the flood took care t' embark,
And save his carcase in the ark;   *1090*
But as it fares in state and church,
Left his constituents in the lurch.

F I N I S

NOTES
FOR THE AID
OF THE READER

THE NOTES FOR THIS EDITION ARE PROVIDED FOR THE AID OF the reader not thoroughly familiar with the life and history of the American eighteenth century or with the literary and Biblical learning that Trumbull assumed in his readers. For the most part they are designed only to explain direct references in the poem. No attempt has been made at critical comment or at identifying literary parallels that Trumbull probably had in mind. The notes printed with the text are Trumbull's own, and appear in the original edition.

The notes here are deliberately brief, following the assumption that most readers of Trumbull want only the necessary information to understand the poem, and that it is better to chance the omission of one or two small points for a particular reader than to offer so great a mass of information that following the notes becomes a chore. The editor hopes that he has given precise enough information that any reader who wants to pursue a point further will be able to find it in standard reference works. *M'Fingal* was edited by Benson J. Lossing in 1860 with extensive and even chatty notes, and the interested reader will find greater elaboration of many points there, although he must be on his guard against errors in the notes as well as in the text. *The Progress of Dulness* has not been published in an annotated edition before except for the occasional comments in contemporary printings.

PROGRESS OF DULNESS

Part I

Titlepage. wore a wig: a wig was then a part of the formal clerical dress.

Titlepage. *Daries, daries*: "An ancient charm against broken limbs." See note for line 156.

46. Lillie: William Lily's Latin grammar was the standard textbook of the day.

50. Tully: the popular name then for Marcus Tullius Cicero.

95. *tardes* and *egresses*: terms used at college for entering late and leaving before the conclusion of service.

156. *Pliny*'s rhymes for broken bones: magic charms to cure broken bones, of the sort given on the title page of this part. Trumbull seems to have ascribed the charms to the wrong writer. Pliny in the *Natural History*, Book 28, ch. 3 even attacks the validity of charms. Marcus Cato in the *De Agri Cultura*, CLX, however, offers two such charms which Trumbull apparently has coalesced for his motto: "Motas uaeta daries dardares astataries dissunapiter," and "Huat haut haut istasis tarsis ardannabou dannaustra."

182. In din of battle: that is, in theological disputation.

258. learns to construe and to read: diplomas were then in Latin.

314. What *Poole* explain'd, or *Henry* wrote: Matthew Poole (1624–79) and Matthew Henry (1662–1714) wrote well-known expositions and annotations of the Bible.

333. like *Minerva*: the daughter of Jove who sprang full-grown from her father's head.

342. The future dialogue: theological controversy was often written in the form of dialogues.

372. book of common places: a notebook in which the owner

copies out passages he would like to keep; a common custom of earlier ages.

377. deist's scoffs: deism, or the new rationalistic rejection of revelation combined with belief in God as a first cause only, was considered a near neighbor to atheism by the orthodox.

426. those statues once that spoke at *Rome*: see Juvenal, Satire I, where "marmora clamant," or the marble statues cry aloud.

427. *Livy's* ox: for an account of this portent see Livy's history, Book 28, ch. 11.

447. glib-tongu'd *Merc'ry*: In his Greek form of Hermes, Mercury put Argus of the hundred eyes to sleep by talking to him.

PROGRESS OF DULNESS

Part II

Titlepage. Receipt: in its older meaning of "recipe" or "formula."

Titlepage. *Peripaetia* and *Catastrophe*: pedantic dramatic terms for a sudden change of fortune and the change which produces the final event of a drama.

Preface. nem. con.: "nemine contradicente," no one dissenting.

Preface. Separatist: one who advocates ecclesiastical separation, or a sect separated from the principal church.

Preface. Sandemanian: a member of a religious sect developed by Robert Sandeman (1718–71), an off-spring from the Scottish Glassites.

Preface. Arminians: followers of the doctrine of James Arminius or Harmensen, Dutch Protestant theologian who opposed Calvin, especially on predestination.

93. vice for sale: a reference to the old sale of indulgences by the Roman Catholic Church.

238. *Rochester* and *Tristram Shandy*: the poetry of the Earl of Rochester and Sterne's *Tristram Shandy* were considered almost indecent, and were full of double-entendres. Both were popular.

250. nothing can be known: David Hume, the Scottish philosopher of skepticism, held that nothing can be known by the mind but its own "impressions" and "ideas."

322. their ears: the old penalty for counterfeiting was loss of ears.

374. *Tully*'s rule: in *De Oratore,* XXV.

391. may game: merry-making, sport, foolery; also, a laughing-stock.

394. *Pro meritis*: for his merits; the traditional phrase of the college diploma.

403. fire electric: static electricity.

451. Quoted from *Pope*: "Men, some to business, some to pleasure take;/ But every woman is at heart a rake." *Epistle II; To a Lady.*

471. climate: that is, climate of opinion.

PROGRESS OF DULNESS

Part III

Titlepage. *quaeq; ipse*: "those tragic events that I myself saw, and in which I played a large part." *Aeneid*, II, 5–6.

Preface. *Juvenal*: in Satire 6.

Preface. *Rowe*: Mrs. Elizabeth Singer Rowe, pious English poet of the early century.

27. *Joan of Nokes*: Joan was the traditional name for a country girl; Nokes, a name for a ninny or fool.

127. airpump: early device for creating a vacuum.

156. mint and cummin: aromatic herb and spice used in cooking.

171. catgut: here, a coarse cloth often used as stiffening.

185. tentstitch: a method of embroidery.

248. tuckers: pieces of lace or the like worn within or around the top of the bodice.

272. Th' opposing galleries: young men and women were then seated apart in opposing church galleries.

278. kissing-strings: bonnet strings made long to tie under the chin.

282. training bands: organized groups of local militia or citizen-soldiers.

370. trine and quartile: terms of astrology.

392. *Pamela*: the heroine of Samuel Richardson's *Pamela, or Virtue Rewarded.*

398. *Grandison,* or *Lovelace*: the heroes of Richardson's *Sir Charles Grandison* and *Clarissa.*

402. cits: slang abbreviation of "citizens"; usually applied to city men or generally men about town.

547. stiver: a small coin; originally a Dutch coin worth about two cents.

566. *in forma pauperis*: the legal state in which one is allowed, because of poverty, to sue or defend in court without paying costs.

666. *Christian*: Christian in John Bunyan's *Pilgrim's Progress*.

680. in fam'd romance: Don Quixote and Sancho Panza in Cervantes' *Don Quixote*.

M ' F I N G A L

Titlepage. Ergo non satis: "Therefore it is not enough to make the hearer grin, although there is some merit in that. Brevity is needed, that the thought may run on without becoming entangled in verbiage that weighs upon wearied ears. And a style is needed, now grave now gay, in keeping with the role, now of orator now of poet, sometimes of the urbane wit who keeps his strength under control and husbands it with wisdom. Ridicule often settles a matter of importance more forcefully and effectively than grave severity." Horace, *Satires*, Book I, Satire 10.

M ' F I N G A L

Canto I

11. Percy: Lord Percy, commander of British troops at the skirmish at Lexington, descendant of the Earl Percy killed in the storied battle of Chevy Chase.

31. King: George III, 1760–1820.

33. Jacobite: a supporter of the Stuart pretender to the crown in the Scottish-English political wars of the recent past.

44. Bute and Mansfield: the Earl of Bute was a Scottish minister of George III, and Prime Minister from 1762–63. The Earl of Mansfield was Lord Chief Justice from 1756–88.

61. Dodona: the ancient Greek oracle.

94. Stentor: the Greek herald whose voice was louder than fifty men.

139. pulpit stairs: the town meeting is being held in the church.

146. Merc'ry's wand: Mercury, messenger of the gods and patron of eloquence and rogues, was pictured with wings on his cap and feet and carrying a staff entwined with serpents in his hand.

160. Aeolus: classical ruler of the winds, which he held in a great cave.

202. break and come upon the town: go bankrupt and become a public charge.

214. grand Climact'ric: the sixty-third year; traditionally the year in which great changes in the body occur.

222. Beth'lem: St. Mary of Bethlehem was the most famous of the English lunatic asylums.

236. Pope Joan: the legend is that in the ninth century a woman long disguised as a monk was elected Pope.

250. North: Lord North, Prime Minister 1770–82.

276. Elijah's prophets: see I Kings XVIII.

292. Gage: Thomas Gage, Commander in Chief of the British forces in America, 1763–75, royal governor of Massachusetts, 1774–75.

294. *Posse Comitatus*: a body of citizens summoned to preserve the law.

300. barber's blocks: wooden forms to hold wigs.

348. *Entry sur disseisin*: possession by dispossession or ousting of another.

360. Addressers and Protesters: citizens who at the beginning of hostilities formally "addressed" the royal government in support, and who "protested" against the resolves and actions of the revolutionists.

410. *carte & tierce*: fencing terms; positions of parry and thrust.

442. Barak and Deborah: see Judges V, 5.

454. Tophet was ordain'd: see Isaiah XXX, 33.

463. shoeball: a ball of waterproofing used on shoes.

466. fuller's earth: an absorbent clay used for removing grease from cloth.

468. sinning under licence: an allusion to the sale of indulgences in the early Roman Catholic Church.

512. Rivington: James Rivington, printer of the *Royal Gazette*, a Tory paper of New York.

514. Brush, Cooper, Wilkins, Chandler, Booth: notorious loyalists of the day.

517. Massachusettensis: pen name of Daniel Leonard, author of a series of Tory essays in the Boston papers, 1774–75.

531. Hutchinson: Thomas Hutchinson, royal Lieutenant Governor of Massachusetts 1758–71, Chief Justice 1760–65, Governor 1771–73.

540. Mills, Hicks, mother Draper: printers of Tory papers in Boston.

552. public fast: June 1, 1774, the day the oppressive measures of the Boston Port Bill went into effect, was declared a day of public fasting in Massachusetts.

580. Oliver: Peter Oliver, royal Chief Justice of Massachusetts 1771–74, although not a lawyer by education.

582. mandamus: command from a higher power to a lower to perform its duty. In 1774 the council of Massachusetts was made appointive rather than elective, and was often called the Mandamus Council.

586. Murray, Ruggles, Edson, Thomas, Loring, Pepp'rell, Browne, Erving: all Tories and members of the hated Mandamus Council.

606. Gray: Harrison Gray, royal Receiver General of Massachusetts, and a member of the Mandamus Council.

612. Lord Dartmouth: appointed royal Secretary of State for the colonies in 1772.

614. prime saint: Governor Hutchinson, whose letters to the ministry apparently urging curtailment of American liberties were discovered and published, destroying his public character.

662. sav'd him: General Gage refused to allow Whigs to leave the city of Boston after the battles at Lexington and Concord, keeping them almost as hostages for the protection of the city against the revolutionists under the command of General Putnam.

684. *duress per minas*: constraint by threats; illegal pressure to perform an act.

686. feathers, tar and lib'rty-poles: tall poles inscribed "Liberty" were erected about the colonies as symbols of protest and as rallying points for patriots. Here Tories were occasionally tarred and feathered.

704. broad-alleys: in the early Puritan church sinners were required to stand in the aisle or "broad alley" to name their offenses and ask pardon.

M'FINGAL

Canto II

38. Primate: William Laud, Archbishop of Canterbury 1633–1640, Anglican foe of the Puritans.

44. *causa sine qua non*: an indispensable condition.

52. your foes: the French in the French and Indian War.

56. o'erpaid your quota: the American colonies furnished more than their quota of troops and expenses for the war.

76. throw in your mite: the Crown insisted that the American colonies help support the British troops sent to preserve the peace.

130. Sir Jeffery: Sir Jeffrey Amherst, Commander in Chief of British forces in America, 1758–60; Governor General of British North America, 1760–63.

135. Col'nel Grant: Col. James Grant, British officer in the French and Indian War; later one of Howe's generals in the Revolution.

158. sour small-beer: the legend was that a lion's roar would turn small beer sour.

170. Van's *Delenda est Carthago*: after the Boston Tea Party a Mr. Venn, member of Parliament, applied Cato's denunciation: "Carthage must be destroyed."

190. Guy Carlton and Guy Johnson: Carlton was Governor of Canada during the American Revolution; Johnson was a British Indian agent who helped to raise the Indians against the Americans during the war.

192. Guy of Warwick: British hero of romance; slew the Dun cow, a great man-killing beast.

260. a Fish: see Matthew XVII, 27.

262. sav'd his master: see Numbers XXII.

264. Preserv'd old Rome: the familiar story of the cackling geese on the Capitoline Hill that awakened the Roman sentinels at the approach of the Gauls.

267. So Frogs . . . And Lice: see Exodus VIII.

273. statuary: obsolete for sculptor.

285. such a dance: the retreat from Lexington and Concord.

291. Col'nel Nesbitt: a particularly hated British officer in Boston; said to have tarred and feathered one country man for buying a gun that Nesbitt sold him.

304. Calig'la's valiant deed: the story is that the Emperor Caligula charged the waters of the English channel with his troops and brought back cockle shells in triumph to Rome as spoils of the victory.

327. Leslie: Colonel Alexander Leslie, who in 1775 led a small expedition by sea to Salem, Mass., where by negotiation he refused to allow battle to begin.

436. Mystic river: the river flows past Boston itself.

444. de'el . . . did the swine: see Matthew VIII, 28–32.

448. Howe, Clinton and Burgoyne: three generals who came to America in the same ship in 1775. General William Howe replaced Gage as Commander in Chief.

475. wave-off'rings: the offerings which by the Levitical law were "waved" by the priest when presented in sacrifice. See Leviticus VIII, 27, 29.

492. in uniform: that is, in tar and feathers. The lack of uniforms for the Continental army was a source of ridicule for the British; and Nesbitt's propensity to tar and feathers was a source of hatred for the Americans.

500. rob and plunder: the British navy as well as army was used to forage for supplies along the coast.

530. Graves: Admiral Samuel Graves, commander of the British fleet.

532. Wallace: Sir James Wallace, commander of the small fleet on station off New England.

537. Sandemanian: a religious sect that believed in the coming of the Millennium in a few years.

546. remainder-men in tail: those who hold the right to succeed to a position or property on the death of the holder and to hold it in entail; that is, to have the right to pass it on only to direct heirs.

572. Sisera: see Judges V, 20.

597. that new world: see Revelation XXI.

604. Justice Quorum: loosely used for justice of the peace.

616. Vassals: John Vassal of Cambridge was a well known Tory. Probably a pun intended here as well.

646. tide-waiters: customs officers who boarded ships to prevent evasion of regulations.

682. Abel's from the ground: see Genesis IV, 10.

693. Georgian shores: the province of Georgia had not yet joined the union when this section of the poem was first written.

782. pulpit-canopy: the sounding-board or overhanging cover to be found over many older pulpits.

785. Destinies: the Parcae or fatal sisters: Clotho spun the thread of life; Lachesis doled it out; Atropos cut it off.

802. lecture-day: the week day on which a sermon was preached outside of the regular order of services. By Trumbull's day these sermons were sparsely attended.

M'FINGAL

Canto III

11. Brobdignagian: Brobdingnag is the land of the giants in Swift's *Gulliver's Travels*.

12. Satan's walking-staff: Trumbull was probably thinking of Satan's spear in Book I of *Paradise Lost*.

28. Circe: Homer's enchantress, whose cup turned men into swine.

30. ichor: in classical mythology, the fluid in the veins of the gods.

34. bucket-men: members of fire companies who supplied water in leather buckets for the other fire fighters.

55. Scottish laird and laddie: the Scotch were looked upon with great suspicion by Americans at the time, and were generally associated in the popular mind with Jacobinism and catholicism.

60. Jewish pole in Edom: see Numbers XXI, 9.

61. brazen snake of Moses: again see Numbers XXI, 9. The "or" is epexegetic; that is, it adds a further explanation.

78. scale of depreciation: Congress determined the degree of depreciation of the Continental paper currency by a "scale of depreciation."

80. Jewish jubilee: every fiftieth year the ancient Jews were supposed to hold a national festival at which all debts were cancelled and crimes forgiven.

81. like Aaron's calves: see Exodus XXXII.

82. jurisdictions of white staves: some judges appointed by the crown were driven out of office at the beginning of the war by crowds carrying white staves as symbols of their authority.

121. goose: a tailor's iron.

166. Bacon's brazen head: one of the legends about Roger

Bacon, 13th century philosopher, was that he possessed a human head of brass that spoke oracular wisdom.

172. Trinclo: Trinculo in *The Tempest*.

237. in the suds: the popular belief at the time was that after the Boston Tea Party Governor Hutchinson ran for his life, half shaved and still "in the suds."

255. Smith's weathercock: William Smith, Chief Justice of New York, kept shifting his allegiance in indecision. In 1778 he finally settled on the loyalist side and was appointed Chief Justice of Canada in 1786.

262. Belzebub: when unpopular men were burned in effigy, a figure representing the devil was often burned at the same time.

266. Tryon: William Tryon, royal Governor of North Carolina 1765–71, where he put down the revolt of the "Regulators" with great severity; royal Governor of New York 1771–76; during the war he took command of a group of loyalists.

268. Galloway: Joseph Galloway, Pennsylvania patriot who in 1776 became an active loyalist. On his leaving for England he was mysteriously sent a box containing a halter.

293. Dagon: see 1 Samuel V, 1–5.

295. Jericho's proud wall: see Joshua VI.

381. on the bench: in New England at that time judges on the bench carried swords.

472. Hatchel-teeth: the metal brush-like teeth of an instrument used for combing flax.

495. Murray: John Murray, member of the Mandamus Council who fled to Canada in 1776.

496. Williams: Israel Williams, member of the Mandamus Council. One night a mob locked him in a closed room with the chimney stopped and smoked him for several hours until he signed a recantation of his Tory beliefs.

497. Oliver: Andrew Oliver, as royal distributor of stamps was hanged in effigy by a mob in 1765 and forced to take an oath of resignation; appointed Lieutenant Governor of Massachusetts in 1771 although the General Court petitioned the Crown to remove him.

500. stole his types: in 1775 the Sons of Liberty destroyed the press and carried off the types of James Rivington, Tory printer of New York.

571. Maia's son: Mercury, generally represented with wings

on his cap and heels.

573. Milton's six wing'd angel: see *Paradise Lost* V, 277–85.

576. Gorgon or Chimera: Gorgon, any of the three sisters who had snakes for hair and whose glance turned the beholder to stone; Chimera, a monster represented with a lion's head, a goat's body, and a serpent's tail.

582. Duumvirate: in Roman custom, the union of two men in one office.

M'FINGAL

Canto IV

94. the last rebellion: the Scotch rebellion of 1745 in attempt to bring the Stuart pretender to the British throne. In America the Scotch were popularly associated with toryism.

106. Orpheus: the figure of classical mythology who went down to the underworld to rescue his wife, Eurydice.

108. realms of Erebus and Orcus: the classical underworld.

112. Old Adam saw: in *Paradise Lost* XI.

123. the well of Bute: an allusion to Lord Bute, the Scottish minister of George III.

125. euphrasy and rue: formerly used in making eye wash.

140. Montgom'ry: General Richard Montgomery, who captured Montreal in 1775.

143. Bemus' Heights: the battle of Bemis Heights, N.Y., where Generals Gates and Arnold defeated Burgoyne in 1777.

145. Bennington: the skirmish at Bennington, Vt., in which one of Burgoyne's expeditions was defeated in 1777.

146. Stony-Point: a British fortress on the Hudson captured by General Anthony Wayne in 1779.

148. Trenton's shore: the famous battle in which Washington defeated and captured a Hessian garrison by crossing the Delaware on Christmas night, 1776.

153. Princeton plains: the battle immediately following Trenton in which Washington defeated Cornwallis' commander Mawhood after drawing Cornwallis out of position.

157. Pennsylvanian shore: the bloody battles of Brandywine Creek and Germantown in Pennsylvania in 1777, in which both sides lost heavily.

163. Dunmore's negro band: in 1775 Lord Dunmore, royal

Governor of Virginia, enlisted negro slaves in the army. They were soon defeated.

166. The Scotch M'Donalds: in 1776 a military force of sixteen hundred loyalist Scotsmen under the command of Donald Macdonald was recruited in North Carolina. The group was soon defeated and dispersed at the battle of Moore's Creek.

167. King's Mountain: battle in South Carolina, 1780, in which a large detachment of Cornwallis's army was defeated.

169. Tarlton's blust'ring train: shortly after the battle of King's Mountain, Cornwallis's commander Colonel Tarleton was defeated at the Cowpens.

171. Eutaw's fatal springs: the battle of Eutaw Springs, S.C., 1781, in which the American General Greene was defeated but cost the British heavily. One of the last battles of the southern campaign.

182. Berkley's immaterial scheme: George Berkeley, philosopher, offered a destructive criticism of Locke's external or material reality, and found spirit the only real cause or power.

189. Baal: see 2 Kings XI, 18.

254. Satan's surg'ries: see Job II, 1–8.

263–64. in the lap of Loring: Mrs. Joshua Loring, wife of the British commissary of prisons, was a notorious mistress of General Howe.

268. instantaneous breastworks: on the night of March 4, 1776 the Americans threw up fortifications on Dorchester Heights overlooking Boston. Howe and his forces caught by surprise were forced to abandon the city and withdraw to Halifax.

293. our chosen vet'ran band: the army of General Burgoyne descending on New York from Canada in the campaign of 1777.

298. like bees at sound of kettle: it was believed that swarming bees could be directed by beating upon tin pans and kettles.

327. with asses jaw: see Judges XV, 15–16.

329. our vet'ran thousands yield: Burgoyne's surrender at Saratoga, Oct. 17, marked the end of the campaign of 1777. Prisoners were marched off to the tune of Yankee Doodle.

343. Macaroni: contemporary epithet for the fop or dandy who derived his style and graces from the Italian.

344. Phoebus and Bellona: the god of light and the arts, and the god of war; the graces and the terrors.

363. Prior's wit: Matthew Prior wrote his *Alma; or The Progress of the Mind* while under arrest.

365. Raleigh fast in prison: Sir Walter Raleigh wrote his *History of the World* in the Tower of London.

367. Wilkes: John Wilkes (1725–97), the violent and vocal center of the liberal political agitation in England during the second half of the century. He was imprisoned for libel for a short while. By the end of his life he had lost public favor.

386. small change, like simple Prescott: the British General Richard Prescott was twice captured and exchanged by the Americans.

411. Loring: Joshua Loring, British commissary of prisons, husband of the Mrs. Loring who appears earlier in the Canto as the mistress of General Howe.

426. Milton's lazar house: see *Paradise Lost* XI, 477–95.

448. Carlton's coaxing plan: Sir Guy Carleton, governor of Canada, treated his American prisoners leniently after their unsuccessful attack on Quebec in 1775.

462. pestilence and death: Howe was popularly accused of deliberately spreading disease about the country.

473. Kishon's brook: see Judges IV, 7.

490. Lybian Ammon: Egyptian deity, identified with the Roman Jupiter; in Lybian form represented with horns.

494. th'idol Bel: the Biblical Baal.

497. Moloch: see Leviticus XVIII, 21 and XX, 2–5.

514. Pharaoh's vision: see Genesis XLI.

520. Clive: Robert Lord Clive (1725–74), the general and governor who subdued India and added it to the British empire. He died by his own hand.

538. Clinton, Vaughan and Tryon: British commanders considered ruthless military marauders during the war.

543. Samson's foxes: see Judges XV, 4–5.

610. The Trojan: Aeneas.

612. gingerbread: on his descent into the underworld, Aeneas slipped by Cerberus, the monster guarding the entrance, by throwing him—as Trumbull indicates in his note—"melle soporatum et medicatis frugibus offam," a morsel drowsy with honey and drugged meal. *Aeneid,* Book 6, line 420.

614. Johnstone: George Johnstone, former governor of West Florida, sent in 1778 as one of the commissioners of the Crown to negotiate a settlement of conflicts with America. Funds for

bribery were available to the commission.

622. petticoated politician: Mrs. Elizabeth Ferguson of Philadelphia, through whom the commission attempted to bribe General Joseph Reed, Washington's Adjutant General.

628. Arnold: General Benedict Arnold, the traitor who schemed to turn West Point over to the British.

650. Prison-bars: a children's game.

664. successor: General Sir Henry Clinton replaced Howe in May, 1778.

682. moonlight marches: in 1778 Clinton abandoned Philadelphia and began the march to New York. Washington caught him at the indecisive battle of Monmouth Court House in New Jersey, and that night while the Americans slept Clinton continued his march to New York. Later in official dispatches Clinton spoke of taking advantage of the moonlight, although the new moon was said by patriots to have set before he began his march.

709. British Joshua stay'd the moon: see Joshua X, 13.

731. in firm alliance joins: on Feb. 6, 1778, France and the United States signed a treaty of commerce and friendship and a treaty of alliance.

734. his sails innum'rous: in 1778 a French fleet under the count D'Estaing was sent to aid the Americans. In 1779 the fleet also defeated a British fleet in the West Indies, and captured several islands.

753. Charlestown: General Benjamin Lincoln, one of the officers under Gates who had helped to defeat Burgoyne, surrendered Charleston, S.C. to the British in May, 1780.

761. the southern realms: after the fall of Charleston, the British under Cornwallis soon conquered the Carolinas and Georgia, and generally controlled the South up to Virginia.

781. Rodney's self among th' Eustations: in 1780 Admiral George Rodney captured and sacked the Dutch colony of St. Eustatius, previously a source of neutral supplies for the Americans. The American colonies were righteously incensed.

790. Greene: General Nathaniel Greene in 1781 recaptured the greater part of the South for the American colonies.

824. Sees ruin wake on ev'ry side: the French fleet under De Grasse, Washington's army, and the French forces under Rochambeau combined to force the surrender of Cornwallis at Yorktown, Va., Oct. 19, 1781.

826. Burgoyn'd: after Burgoyne's surrender of his army at Saratoga, his name became synonomous with complete surrender.

827. Cadmus: in the *Metamorphoses*, Cadmus, the founder of Thebes, sowed the teeth of a dragon he had killed, only to see them spring up instantly as a crop of armed warriors.

848. Tyburn's stage: Tyburn was the most famous place of public execution in England.

874. sin-offering: an offering in repentance and expiation of sin; see Leviticus IV, 2–3.

876. a recreant cargo: during negotiations for the surrender at Yorktown, Cornwallis was allowed to send one ship load of loyalist troops to safety in New York.

902. Like Mercy's door in proclamations: British proclamations before and during the war repeatedly used such expressions as "The door of mercy is still open," and "The door of mercy will soon be shut."

912. drest in plumes: the "Genius of America" was often pictured in Indian feather headdress. Here Trumbull is joking too about Tories in tar and feathers.

924. Mansfield's sentence: as Lord Chief Justice, Mansfield represented the English Law that transported felons to the colonies.

928. *ne exeat*: a writ that forbids leaving a region or a country.

942. "Regulation" and "Tender": the acts of the various state legislatures to "regulate" prices and to make Continental paper money legal "tender."

944. "The faith of all th' United States": the pledge of Congress on the Continental paper money.

963. Jove fell: Jupiter came to Danae, to make her the mother of Perseus, in the form of a golden shower through the roof of her prison.

968. tallies cast by Charles the second: in 1672 Charles II cancelled all payments of assignations on the revenue; in effect the exchequer was closed without paying its debts.

969. Law's famed Mississipi schemes: John Law of Edinburgh promoted in France in the early part of the century a Mississippi trading company. The scheme soon collapsed, ruining many investors.

970. Southsea dreams: a similar speculative scheme in Eng-

land, "The South Sea Company," that had a similar ruinous end.

972. Philos'pher's stone: the long-sought agent that would transmute base metals to gold.

979. essoign: legal term for an excuse, particularly for not appearing in court.

984. counterfeit his art: counterfeit Continental bills were printed and circulated by the British during the war.

994. the true Mosaic lice: see Exodus VIII, 1–19.

1031. crasis: constitution, temperament.

1072. the family of Lot: see Genesis XIX, 15–26.

The Satiric Poems of John Trumbull
has been printed in Baskerville and Bulmer types by
The Printing Division of
THE UNIVERSITY OF TEXAS
Design by Kim Taylor
1962

CPSIA information can be obtained
at www.ICGtesting.com
Printed in the USA
LVHW080441280922
729469LV00010B/260